Tax Guide 503

DISAGREEING WITH THE IRS

by

Holmes F. Crouch
Tax Specialist

Published by

Allyear Tax Guides

20484 Glen Brae Drive
Saratoga, CA 95070

ISBN 0-944817-47-5

LCCN 97-75302

Printed in U.S.A.

Series 500
Audits & Appeals

Tax Guide 503

DISAGREEING WITH THE IRS

For other titles in print, see page 224.

The author: **Holmes F. Crouch**
For more about the author, see page 221.

PREFACE

If you are a knowledge-seeking **taxpayer** looking for information, this book can be helpful to you. It is designed to be read — from cover to cover — in less than eight hours. Or, it can be "skim-read" in about 30 minutes.

Either way, you are treated to **tax knowledge** . . . *beyond the ordinary*. The "beyond" is that which cannot be found in IRS publications, FedWorld on-line services, tax software programs, or on CD-ROMs.

Taxpayers have different levels of interest in a selected subject. For this reason, this book starts with introductory fundamentals and progresses onward. You can verify the progression by chapter and section in the table of contents. In the text, "applicable law" is quoted in pertinent part. Key phrases and key tax forms are emphasized. Real-life examples are given . . . in down-to-earth style.

This book has 12 chapters. This number provides depth without cross-subject rambling. Each chapter starts with a head summary of meaningful information.

To aid in your skim-reading, informative diagrams and tables are placed strategically throughout the text. By leafing through page by page, reading the summaries and section headings, and glancing at the diagrams and tables, you can get a good handle on the matters covered.

Effort has been made to update and incorporate all of the latest tax law changes that are *significant* to the title subject. However, "beyond the ordinary" does not encompass every conceivable variant of fact and law that might give rise to protracted dispute and litigation. Consequently, if a particular statement or paragraph is crucial to your own specific case, you are urged to seek professional counseling. Otherwise, the information presented is general and is designed for a broad range of reader interests.

The Author

INTRODUCTION

The Internal Revenue Service (IRS) touches — and bruises — the lives of more people in the United States than any other single agency of government. Approximately 130,000,000 (130 million) persons — called "taxpayers" — are affected each year by its rules, regulations, and tax collection procedures. The nearest government agency affecting large numbers of people is the Social Security Administration. It touches — and assists — approximately 35,000,000 (35 million) persons (called "recipients").

In terms of pure pocketbook matters, there is no agency in the world with the power of the IRS to tax, levy, and seize money against one's will. Over the 85 years since inception of the federal income tax in 1913, the IRS has become a law unto itself. Technically, it answers to the Joint Committee on Taxation. But, in reality, it answers to no one: not to the President; not to the Congress; not to the Courts. And it certainly doesn't respond with any empathy towards injured taxpayers in a manner that elicits credibility in itself nor respect for government overall.

After all annual returns are filed, the IRS contacts (by computer) approximately 40,000,000 taxpayers each year. Many of the contacts are ordinary arithmetic corrections, refunds, and the pointing out of oversights and errors in various tax forms filed. But most of the contacts are **demands** for more money: more tax . . . plus penalties . . . plus interest. In its obsession with power — called "collection enforcement" — the IRS's demands too often are erroneous, egregious, and way off target.

To illustrate what we mean, here's a TRUE STORY. On April 27, 1995, taxpayer AFL (true initials) went to pick up his paycheck from his employer. Instead, payroll handed him IRS Form 668: *Notice of Levy on Wages, Salary, and Other Income.* The total amount due was $82,128.61. Bursting with anger and disbelief, he read the "details":

1987	19,586.52 tax	2,290.02 additions	21,876.54
1988	52,218.90 tax	8,033.17 additions	60,252.07
			$82,128.61

"There is no way I owe this amount," AFL said to the payroll rep. "Sorry," she responded. "We have no choice but to take each of your paychecks and turn them over to the IRS until the entire $82,000+ is paid. You'll have to contact the IRS yourself to arrange otherwise."

On December 20, 1995, the IRS confirmed that AFL owed only as follows:

1987	$ 0
1988	$298.25

In the meantime, the IRS had seized $18,168.53 of AFL's various-year tax refunds and wages!

When the IRS demands more money, you have three options. **One**, you can agree in full and pay (in full). **Two**, you can agree partially, and disagree partially. **Three**, you can disagree in full . . . and protest appropriately.

Yes, you **can** disagree legitimately with the IRS. Your right to do so is "guaranteed" by *Taxpayer Bill of Rights 1* (enacted November 10, 1988) and by *Taxpayer Bill of Rights 2* (enacted July 30, 1996). Additional such rights are being contemplated by Congress. The playing field is not yet level.

As always, one's "rights" of any kind are not unlimited. Before you can disagree legitimately with the IRS, you must have filed a relevant-year tax return. Thereafter, your disagreeing actions must be in the form of **written** objections, notices, amendments, protests, appeals, and complaints. Oral disagreements are ineffective.

Instructing you in the proper disagreeing manner is what this book is all about. Most of the actions we address are sanctioned by official policy, by the intent of Congress, and by limited protections in the Internal Revenue Code.

CONTENTS

1

OFFICIAL IRS POLICY

The "Statement Of Principles" By The IRS
Proclaims Its Dedication To Improving Its
Service, Fairness, And Courtesy When
Determining Your Federal Tax . . . And
Collecting It. In An Open Letter To Over
130,000,000 (130 Million) Taxpayers Each
Year, The IRS Commissioner Confirms These
Lofty Goals. So, Too, Did Congress In 1988
And 1996 When It Enacted The "Taxpayer Bill
Of Rights." Most Such Policy Efforts Are PR
Window Dressing. None Of The Above
Changes The PRESUMPTION OF CORRECT-
NESS By The IRS . . . In Whatever It Does.

The mission of the IRS is to collect money. Its mission is to collect maximum money. Its mission is to collect maximum money from all U.S. taxpayers . . . worldwide. (Here, the term "U.S. taxpayers" means: U.S. citizens, whether resident or nonresident **and** U.S. residents, whether citizen or noncitizen.) This is the primary mission: collecting M-O-N-E-Y and directing it into the Federal Treasury.

Its subordinate mission is to continuously expand the IRS bureaucracy for enforcement of its money-collecting goals. This is where all the danger lies. Bureaucracy begets endless rules and regulations, tons of forms and instructions, and computer-assessed penalties. Bureaucracy also begets a body of personnel on the public payroll who are more obsessed with their power — to tax and destroy — than with their dedication to public service. This is the seamy side of Tax Life, USA.

Starkly stated, the IRS is a gigantic money-funneling bureaucracy. Its collection tentacles reach deep into all productive pockets, skim the offtop best, and pass that money through its various "processing centers." From these centers, the discharging outlets feed directly to the U.S. Treasury. This receptacle is the *black hole* of Big Government.

Compare this stark reality with the official pronouncement of the IRS's mission. The official statement is—

The purpose of the Internal Revenue Service is to collect the proper amount of tax revenue at the least cost; serve the public by continually improving the quality of our products and services; and perform in a manner warranting the highest degree of public confidence in our integrity, efficiency, and fairness.

Noble words, but unattainable in practice.

In this introductory chapter, therefore, we want to familiarize you with the various statements of principles of (official) IRS policy. In this familiarization, we will also review those Congressional principles set forth in the 1988 and 1996 "Taxpayer Bill of Rights." We want you to keep these official policy pronouncements in mind when you encounter the frontline demands of IRS computers and IRS personnel.

Mission Impossible

Each year, the IRS processes well over 130,000,000 (130 million) individual tax returns. It employs about 125,000 persons to do so. It uses more than 4,000 computer software programs. It publishes nearly 700 different tax forms. It interprets some 1,800 tax laws, and administers about 15,000 Treasury regulations.

All of this constitutes a complex, mind-boggling system of tax assessment and collection. The system requires substantial knowledge and expertise, not only by the IRS, but also by tax professionals and the taxpaying public. The consequence is that the lofty goals of official policy are impossible to achieve.

Part of the IRS's lofty-goal problem is computer technology. The IRS still hasn't come to grips with the fact that its computer "printouts" are **not** human communicative forms. The monolithic printings are too stereotyped. They lack attention-informing headings and subheadings for identifying the subject matter or issues at hand. The referenced phone numbers for inquiry produce no answers, no human responses, or busy signals. In most cases, one is automatically transferred to other phone numbers. Over 40,000,000 (40 million) unsatisfied inquiries are made each year.

The printouts tend to confuse and intimidate rather than to inform. They generate disgust with the system rather than compliance with it. As a result, the computer printouts negate much of the needed confidence in the IRS.

There's another confidence-negating aspect in the IRS's mission impossible. It is that official clause above: *improving the quality of our products and services*. Any pretense of "quality products and services" is out of context for a government bureaucracy. Every taxpayer knows that the IRS is not a productive enterprise in the creative sense of bettering society. Collecting tax money is a **necessary task** (some would say "evil"), but it is not a noble undertaking by any stretch of words.

Still another reason for its impossible mission is the "attitude problem" within the IRS. Because of its total reliance on computers, total reliance on penalties (for enforcement), and total reliance on its power to say "No," the official *unofficial* internal policy is—

"When in doubt, stick it to the taxpayer. And, while at it, heap maximum penalties upon him (or her, or them), and add daily compounded interest."

When an honest doubt exists, why not give the benefit to the taxpayer? Why "stick it to him"?

If the IRS really wanted to instill taxpayer confidence in its "integrity, efficiency, and fairness" (official words), why not state its mission simply as—

"The purpose of the Internal Revenue Service is to collect the **correct** amount of tax, for the least penalties, at the least cost, with minimum anguish to the taxpaying public."

This, in contrast to official policy, is ATTAINABLE.

Note that we have used the word "correct" to replace the word "proper" in the official mission stated earlier. When dealing with the black hole of Government, the "proper amount" is the maximum amount, whether it is correct or not. The tactics of maximum amount always create maximum pain — and maximum contempt —

for any revenue collection system. Thus, all official statements regarding tax policy should be treated with "proper" skepticism.

The "Heart of Administration"

The IRS publishes a one-page *Statement of Principles of Internal Revenue Tax Administration*. It is printed in poster-size form for posting on the bulletin boards in those regional, district, and field offices of the IRS where taxpayers go. We estimate that there are well over 1,000 of the public postings nationwide. Obviously, the IRS wants all taxpayers to know its stated policy objectives.

The official statement of principles consists of five paragraphs. We'll quote *all* of these paragraphs in full, in a moment. However, we'll do so in two phases. We designate the first three paragraphs as the "heart of administration" phase. We designate the last two paragraphs as the "reasonable and vigorous" phase.

Except for intentional emphasis (in bold type) and the paragraph designations in brackets, the first three paragraphs read exactly as follows:

[1] *The function of the Internal Revenue Service is to administer the Internal Revenue Code. Tax policy for raising revenue is determined by Congress.*

[2] *With this in mind, it is the duty of the Service to carry out that policy **by correctly applying** the laws enacted by Congress; to determine the reasonable meaning of various Code provisions in the light of the Congressional purpose in enacting them; and to perform this work in a fair and impartial manner, **with neither** a government nor a taxpayer point of view.*

[3] *At the **heart** of **administration is interpretation** of the Code. It is the responsibility of each person in the Service, charged with the duty of interpreting the law, to try to find the **true meaning** of the statutory provision and not to adopt a strained construction in the belief that he or she is "protecting the revenue." The revenue is properly protected only when we ascertain and apply the true meaning of the statute.*

As to paragraph [1], there's no ambiguity there. Congress enacts the tax laws; the IRS collects the money. This is straightforward enough.

As to paragraph [2], what is "reasonable meaning"? Can't you surmise? It's *"neither* a government nor a taxpayer point of view." It's the IRS's point of view!

The IRS is neither the government nor the taxpayer. The IRS is a separate body of law unto itself. Congress never said that the IRS's point of view shall prevail. But Congress did not say that the IRS's point of view shall not prevail, either. Thus, by default, Congress has allowed the IRS to become an extraconstitutional power unto its own.

What Is "True Meaning"?

The heartbeat of IRS power is its version of finding the *true meaning* of a tax law. Basically, true meaning is whatever the IRS deems it to be. This edict has evolved from various federal court decisions (mostly the Tax Court) upholding the theory that the IRS is **presumed correct**. The courts have reasoned that, since Congress has in its power the prerogative to define the term "true meaning" in the IR Code, and it has not done so, it has to be presumed that the IRS is correct.

So the lofty policy statement in paragraph [3] above about finding the true meaning of a statute, by not adopting a strained construction of it, is a gross distortion. When push comes to shove between the IRS and the taxpayer, true meaning boils down to nothing more than the personal opinion and whim of the IRS employee interpreting it. In the politics of tax, true meaning is in the mindset of the IRS. It is never in the IRS's heart.

The IRS position is that if an item is not expressly black or expressly white in a tax law or regulation, it must interpret against the taxpayer. The IRS knows that if it does this often enough, causing pain and anguish to many taxpayers, sooner or later, one or more taxpayers will test the matter in Tax Court. If the court rules occasionally in favor of a taxpayer, the IRS can refuse to acquiesce to that finding.

If numerous taxpayers test the same matter in court, and some of them win, sooner or later the interpretive issue will come to the attention of Congress. Then maybe — just maybe — Congress will amend the law to make it all black or all white. Only then can the true meaning be ascertained.

To win in court, each taxpayer separately must overcome (destroy) the presumption of correctness theory that favors the IRS. This is done through competent evidence that a different finding of true meaning is plausible from that which the IRS asserts. So important is this adversarial burden to true meaning that we present a depiction of it in Figure 1.1.

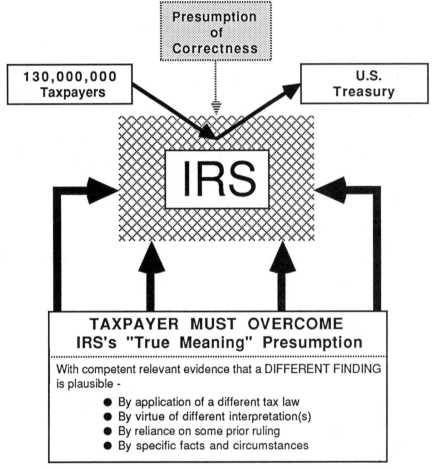

Fig. 1.1 - Burden of Overcoming the "Presumption Theory"

Instead of putting a taxpayer through all of the Figure 1.1 pain, Congress could have — and should have — enacted definitive legislation. For example, it could enact a now *nonexistent* Section 6119: "True Meaning" Defined. Such a new tax code section under existing Miscellaneous Provisions might read as—

> "Whenever it appears that there is an honest doubt in the interpretation of a statute, and the taxpayer presents good faith competent evidence in his own behalf, the issue shall be decided in favor of the taxpayer."

Why does the IRS ALWAYS interpret against a taxpayer?

"Reasonable and Vigorous"?

Let us continue now with paragraphs [4] and [5] of the IRS's Statement of Principles. With instructional emphasis, these paragraphs read in full as—

> [4] *The Service also has the responsibility of applying and administering the law in a **reasonable, practical manner**. Issues should only be raised by examining officers when they have merit, never arbitrarily or for trading purposes. At the same time, the examining officer should never hesitate to raise a **meritorious issue**. It is also important that care be exercised not to raise an issue or to ask a court to adopt a position inconsistent with an established Service position.*

> [5] *Administration should be **both reasonable and vigorous**. It should be conducted with as little delay as possible and with great courtesy and consideration. It should **never try to overreach**, and should be reasonable within the bounds of law and sound administration. It should, however, be vigorous in **requiring compliance** with law and it should be relentless in its attack on unreal tax devices and fraud.*

As to paragraph [4], we get the impression that the IRS knows it has an image problem. The image is that its tax examiners (auditors) are a nit-picky bunch. They arbitrarily raise issues and take intransigent positions to maximize revenue and thereby enhance their promotional status within the IRS. Of course, the IRS says this is not true . . . because all issues raised are "meritorious."

As to paragraph [5], there seems to be a contradiction. How can it be *both* reasonable and vigorous at the same time? Each term negates the other. Being reasonable would not be being vigorous. Being vigorous would not be being reasonable. Whether these two objectives can be executed simultaneously "with great courtesy and consideration," we have our doubts. Particularly so, in view of the IRS's track record of always overreaching.

As to "requiring compliance" in those unreal tax situations (frivolity, fraud, evasion, etc.), we have no quarrel. That's what the IRS is supposed to do. BUT, there's a judgment call problem. The IRS has no objective criteria (checklist type) which its employees must sign "under penalties of perjury," before it stamps down hard on what it perceives to be a noncompliant taxpayer. Personal vendetta and vindictiveness by IRS employees too often come on scene.There are many times when the IRS is "relentless" for the wrong reasons.

Commissioners' Open Letters

Concerned about the IRS's bad public image, every year the Commissioner of Internal Revenue publishes an "open letter" to individual taxpayers. The tone is sincere. At this top level there is an awareness that all is not well in tax wonderland. There is a genuine desire to improve things.

There is reason why the Commissioner is sensitive to public dissatisfaction with the IRS. He/she is appointed by the President and confirmed by the Senate. The President and members of the Senate are elected officials. Electorate-approved officials are more tuned to the grievances of their constituents. Therefore, when selecting candidates for the Commissioner's post, persons with affability and sincerity are preferred.

The practice of open letters started around 1982. New, stringent, compliance rules were enacted at that time and Congress wanted to soft-pedal the harsh measures. The open letter became a vehicle for this soft-pedalling. The letter now appears each year in the Form 1040 Instruction Booklet. There, each Commissioner tries to "reach out" and placate harried taxpayers at tax-filing time.

Here's a sampling from three Commissioners in the 1990s:

Circa 1990 — *Our tax system works because taxpayers are willing to do their part. At IRS our challenge for the 90s is to make the tax system work better for you. . . . This means sending you correspondence only when necessary and making sure that you can conclude your business with the IRS in a single contact, preferably by telephone. We're working to improve, and we promise to continue our efforts to give you the quality of service you have the right to demand from your government.*

/s/ **Fred T. Goldberg, Jr.**

Circa 1992— *As the Commissioner of Internal Revenue, I want to thank you . . . for paying your taxes. We realize that the tax law is complex and sometimes frustrating. We want to do what we can to make tax time easier for you. . . . Our goal is to transform the tax system by the end of this decade. To achieve the excellence in service that you deserve, we are literally "reinventing" the Internal Revenue Service [by] making [ourselves] more efficient and less bureaucratic. As we improve, we also will do a better job of serving our customers, the taxpayers.*

/s/ **Shirley D. Peterson**

Circa 1996 — *The Internal Revenue Service has embarked on several major initiatives that will improve our service to you, the American taxpayer. . . . I want you to know that the"S" in IRS represents a commitment to serve you. We intend to meet your needs and expectations as taxpayers and as customers. . . . We've made real progress, by making it easier to file [your] tax returns electronically, [or] by telephone, [and] by the use of forms 1040EZ. We remain committed to doing even better.*

/s/ **Margaret M. Richardson**

You cannot fault the IRS Commissioners for not trying. They are well-meaning persons: all of them. But they all have one fundamental problem. Between themselves and the taxpaying public, there is an impenetrable barrier of career bureaucrats who frustrate their noble-sounding policies. It is a "power thing" with these career addicts; it has a dooming effect on all Commissioners' efforts. We depict this situation for you in Figure 1.2. As a result, the IRS will always be its own worst enemy. Addiction to power is its core evil.

Hanging onto power over people and their pocketbooks is still the IRS's steadfast goal. Softpedaling this goal is what the "reinventing" is all about.

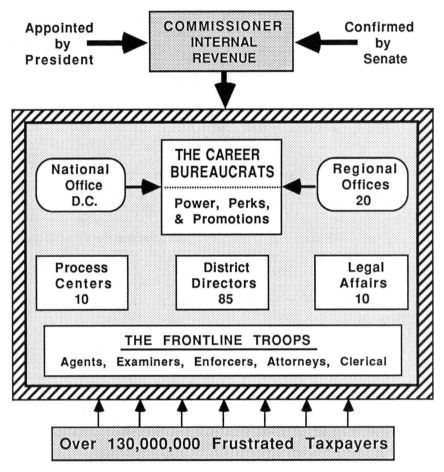

Fig. 1.2 - Impenetrable Bureaucracy Dooming IRS Commissioners

Higher Service Standards

Trying to neutralize the Figure 1.2 barrier, Treasury officials have set forth certain *Customer Service Standards* for the IRS to pursue. These "standards" are listed in the IRS's Form 1040 Instruction Booklet. For the first time ever (in 1996), the Secretary of the Treasury — under whom the IRS operates — displayed his name to the taxpaying public. He stated—

The people of the Treasury Department are dedicated to doing what government should do: Meet the highest standards in serving our fellow Americans.

— Robert Rubin,
Secretary of the Treasury

In all, there are eight such standards, namely:

1. Easier Filing	5. One-Stop Service
2. Access to Information	6. Canceling Penalties
3. Accuracy	7. Resolving Problems
4. Prompt Refunds	8. Simpler Forms

The two cornerstones of these standards are easier filing and simpler forms. The IRS and the Treasury Department want to make it as easy as possible for you to pay as much tax as you are willing to pay. Nothing is said about paying minimum taxes in a simpler way. The "easy filing — simple forms" standard involves electronic filing, joint Federal-state filing, TeleFile, electronic payment transfers, and EZ form designs.

Our words to the wise are as follows:

(1) The simpler the form, the higher the tax.
(2) The easier it is to file, the less are the offsets for deductions, credits, and expenses.

So, don't get too enthralled at rushing your money into the Federal Treasury at the rate of 1.5 trillion dollars ($1,500,000,000) a year . . . a rate which will never decrease.

When rushing to pay too fast and easy, you don't have time to think through alternative strategies for saving taxes. If later you find that you overpaid, you'll have a tough time getting your money back. The term "prompt refund" means only if you file a *complete and accurate return* which is *not selected for further review* (Standard No. 4).

Are Taxpayers "Customers"?

We applaud the efforts of top brass at the IRS and Treasury Department for trying to improve service to their customers. But, really, are taxpayers "customers"?

The term "customer" applies to the competitive world of private business. In such world, there is a choice of products and services among competing provider interests. And the choice is voluntary. There is nothing voluntary about filing a tax return. It is mandatory. If you don't file, a pyramid of penalties and compound interest applies. Nor is there any choice among the many government agencies that dominate U.S. life. There is only one agency — the IRS — with which a tax return can be filed. Consequently, we think it a bit much to address taxpayers as customers.

If taxpayers were really customers of the IRS with free choice, we can cite one fact right off: There are a lot of dissatisfied customers out there! Are their complaints taken seriously? Absolutely not. When there is reasonable doubt in the interpretation of a tax law, is the doubt resolved in favor of the "customer"? Absolutely not.

Therefore, it is a public relations hoax to pretend that taxpayers are customers of the IRS. We don't mind the PR dedication to improving service to taxpayers. But to equate taxpayers with customers just generates more cynicism towards the IRS.

Furthermore, it should be made clear that the IRS's goal of improving service pertains only to clerical and administrative matters. The services targeted for improvement are access to IRS forms and publications, instructions on procedures, refund status, systemic problems (one arm of the IRS not knowing what the other arm is doing), and live telephone assistance . . . IF you can ever get through to a human being.

Few to none of the targeted service improvements have to do with returns processing, selections for audit, disputive tax issues, erroneous tax assessments, collection enforcement, and so on. These are the meaty issues of taxpayer life where most of the agony and concern arise. This is the operations and power arm of the IRS. It consists of career addicts who have an entirely different mindset from those in the clerical and administrative arm of the IRS. As we depict in Figure 1.3, it is as though the IRS were comprised of two entirely different agencies. One is trying to improve its image; the other doesn't give a hoot about its image. It's the "good cop — bad cop" routine. The latter is where the power abusers gravitate.

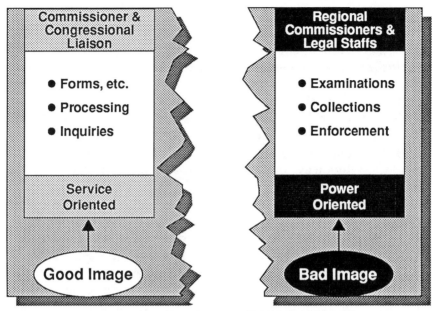

Commissioner & Congressional Liaison	Regional Commissioners & Legal Staffs
• Forms, etc.	• Examinations
• Processing	• Collections
• Inquiries	• Enforcement
Service Oriented	Power Oriented
↑	↑
Good Image	Bad Image

Fig. 1.3 - Our Two Separate IRS "Governments"

"Bill of Rights" Acts

The period of 1982 to 1988 was a time of great revenue magic. Congress had found a way to boost revenues sharply . . . "without raising taxes." The feat was accomplished by authorizing the IRS to pyramid penalties, compound interest, overassess taxpayers, and pursue automatic collections enforcement. Soon, horror stories of the IRS's brutality were released to the press by courageous Congressmen. This set off a wave of public clamor for reining in the IRS. The result was a *Taxpayer Bill of Rights* (enacted November 10, 1988), putting the IRS on notice to change its ways towards taxpayers. The shortcomings of this original Act were addressed in Taxpayer Bill of Rights 2 (enacted July 30, 1996).

Both Acts introduced a few new Internal Revenue Code sections, and amended many of those already in place. Acts 1 and 2 addressed such matters as *Disclosure of taxpayer rights* — during the audit, appeals, refund, and collection process. It mandated that the IRS prepare a "Publication 1": *Your Rights as a Taxpayer* and distribute it to all those whom the IRS contacts.

A particular note in Publication 1 says that—

You are responsible for paying only the correct amount of tax due under the law — no more, no less.

The "correct" amount of tax: what is that? When dealing with the IRS, this is THE core problem. Recall from our Introduction where the IRS levied the taxpayer for $82,128. After much aggravation and dismay to the taxpayer, the correct tax turned out to be $300. Obviously, one cannot rely on the IRS to postulate the correct tax.

Determining the correct tax is unlike that of determining the correct price in a business transaction. If you don't like the price, either you don't buy the product or service, or you go to a competitor for it. If you don't like the tax amount, you either pay it or you disagree with it. If you disagree, there are certain procedures to follow. In the end, you usually wind up paying something . . . whether correct or not. You can't just walk away and decide not to pay.

In the chapters which follow, we want to set the stage for disagreeing properly — and vehemently — with the IRS. Actual procedures will vary, depending on the facts and circumstance of your case. Even so, all disagreements have one feature in common. You cannot start disagreeing until the IRS **contacts you** in some manner. You cannot disagree by refusing to file a return, when required, or by refusing to pay tax, when due. After all, it was your Congressperson and your President who validated (over time) the entire Internal Revenue Code.

2

IMPORTANCE OF RESPONDING

Once Your Return Is Filed, The IRS Has 3 Years Within Which To Question Its Contents. When Questions Do Arise, You Are Sent A CHANGE OF ACCOUNT NOTICE To Your "Address of Record." The Change May Be: (a) More Tax, (b) Less Refund, (c) Penalties, (d) Interest, (e) Additions To Tax, And/Or (f) Other Additions. The IRS Error Rate In These Matters Is Roughly 35%. Therefore, It Is Unimaginably Important That You Review All Changes Carefully, Make Independent Inquiries On Your Own, Then Certify Mail The Documents Necessary To Prove IRS Wrong. If You Do Not Respond, You Have Only Yourself To Blame For The Consequences.

It is fairly common knowledge that every individual, business, or entity who derives income in excess of a specified exemption amount must file a tax return. Whether one files on time or not is not the point. Whether one pays on time or not is not the point. Whether one files a complete return or one which is incomplete is not the point. When required to file, one must file (period!). The "correct tax" — no matter what you think it is, or what the IRS thinks it is — cannot be determined until a return is filed.

Because filing a return is common knowledge, we are assuming for the purposes of this chapter that a return has indeed been filed. (In the next chapter, we'll discuss the consequences of not filing.) Once a return is filed — right or wrong, complete or incomplete — you need take no further action. You've "done your duty" . . .

provided you filed in good faith. The ball now is in the IRS's domain. It is up to the IRS to contact you for whatever reason it may have.

If you filed the wrong form or for the wrong year, the IRS will contact you. If you filed on time but paid late, the IRS will contact you. If you paid on time but filed late, the IRS will contact you. If you filed and paid on time, but omitted some income that was payer-reported to the IRS, you will be contacted. If you filed and paid on time, and claimed deductions and expenses that could be questioned, you will be contacted. If you claim a filing status that is inconsistent with other information on your return, the IRS will contact you.

Our point is that, until the IRS has cause to contact you, there is nothing you can disagree with. It is only *after* you are contacted by the IRS that you can start disagreeing. When we say "start," we mean prompt response to the *initial* contact: not the second, third, or fourth contact down the line. It is the initial contact that is your golden opportunity to set the stage for your disagreeing actions, all the way to the (sometimes) bitter end.

Contents of Notices

When the IRS contacts you expecting a response, the communication is officially designated a *Notice*. For whatever reason, if you fail to respond to a notice, the consequences can be devastating. They are not always so, but they can be. Aware of the potential devastation, the IRS usually tries to make written contact two or three times before it "lowers the boom." This is the sense of what Congress intended by the 1988 Rights Act.

Under the 1988 Act, Section 7522 was added to the tax code. This section is titled: *Content of Tax Due, Deficiency, and Other Notices*. It is one of the shorter tax laws, so we'll quote it to you in full. It reads—

*(a) **General Rule** — Any notice to which this section applies shall describe the basis for, and identify the amounts (if any) of, the **tax due, interest, additional amounts, additions to the tax,** and **assessable penalties** included in such notice. An inadequate*

description under the preceding sentence shall not invalidate such notice. [Emphasis added.]

(b) Notices to Which Section Applies — *This section shall apply to*

    (1) any tax due notice or deficiency notice,

    (2) any notice generated out of any information return matching program, and

    (3) the 1st letter of proposed deficiency which allows the taxpayer an opportunity for administrative review in the IRS Office of Appeals.

This is the extent of official wording. From these words, it should be self-evident that no notice will ever be sent thanking you for filing a return, paying your taxes, or being a good customer/citizen. Any contact with you is for the sole purpose of possibly extracting more money from you. Here, the term "money" includes: *tax, interest, additional amounts, additions to tax, and penalties.* Or, the contact may be for gathering information for subsequent notices of additional amounts due.

The sense of Congress in these money notices is revealed in its Committee Report on P.L. 100-647. The sense behind Section 7522 reads (in part)—

It is the intent of the conferees that all [pertinent] *information be included in the **original** notice sent by IRS; later copies of a particular notice sent to the same taxpayer need not contain* [all such] *information. . . . The conferees believe that all correspondence* [by the IRS] *should be sufficiently clear to enable a taxpayer to understand an IRS question about a tax return, as well as any adjustments or penalties applied.*

The Congressional sense also is that the IRS must provide reasonably adequate time for a taxpayer to respond meaningfully. The expected response time may be 30 days, 60 days, or 90 days, depending on the severity of the tax issue (or issues) raised. Generally, the IRS states in its notice the amount of response time allowed. Unfortunately, the statement is not always crystal clear when, where, and how one must respond.

Consequences of No Response

The IRS is not required to ascertain why no response to a notice was made. It is required, however, to assess tax . . . and collect it. Section 6301: *Collection Authority*, says flat out—

The [IRS] *shall collect the taxes imposed by the internal revenue laws.*

That's it! This is the shortest tax law in the entire 1,800-plus sections of the Internal Revenue Code.

So, what does the IRS do when there is no response to the second and third notices to the same taxpayer?

Answer: It switches from its good image side to its bad image side. Its bad image side is its *collection enforcement* arm. We tried to forewarn you of this in Figure 1.3 (on page 1-13). Collection enforcement takes on the characteristics of the wrath of God.

The first step in collection enforcement is to strip from one's tax return all deductions, expenses, payment credits, dependency exemptions, cost basis, and other adjustments which reduce the tax on the return. The taxable income becomes the sum of all positive entries on the return. The "recomputed" tax is based on single-filer status, even though the taxpayer may be known to the IRS as being married with several children. To the recomputed maximum possible tax, there are added maximum possible penalties, maximum possible interest, and maximum possible additions to tax. The inevitable result is that a correct $100 tax due amount is suddenly magnified to $85,000 or even $185,000. One is then sent a *Final Notice and Demand* — pay in 10 days or else! We depict this process for you in Figure 2.1.

We exemplify the "or else" collection enforcement procedures by exposing two true cases. One is the AFL case cited in our Introduction. Taxpayer AFL was divorced and working in an entirely different city from that of his ex-wife. Although several IRS notices were sent to his former address, the ex-wife threw them

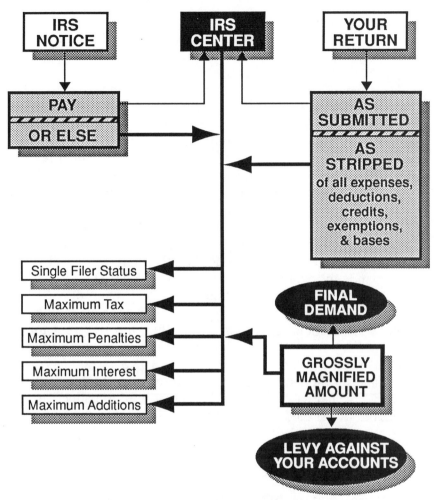

Fig. 2.1 - How IRS Collection Enforcement Procedures Work

all away. She did this intentionally, hoping that the IRS would go after the husband. It did.

As we cited in the Introduction, the correct tax was $300. Nevertheless, the IRS demanded $82,000 and confiscated $18,000 of his wages. This meant that AFL couldn't pay alimony or child support. For this failure, the ex-wife filed a family law complaint against AFL in the County Superior Court.

There are two ironies in the AFL case. One, he actually had overpaid his at-issue tax. He overpaid by about $400 and, thus, was due a refund. However, the refund was never paid because he did not respond to the initial IRS notice.

The second irony was that the pressure and stress of tax collection enforcement, plus the ex-wife's lawsuit for alimony and child support caused his death by massive stroke. Thereafter, all alimony and child support abruptly ceased. This is an example of how embittered spouses can do harm to themselves when relying on the IRS to "punish" their former spouses.

In still another divorce case, taxpayer HEB was unemployed. The spouses were communicative and nonacrimonious. They agreed to sell their residence and "split" the proceeds 60/40 with husband paying off the existing mortgage debt. The house sold in 1988 for $580,000. The wife got $348,000 cash (60% x $580,000); the husband got $64,000 cash (40% x $580,000 − $168,000 mortgage). Because HEB was unemployed, he spent the $64,000 to live on while looking for employment wherever he could find it.

When HEB found employment in 1990, the IRS sent him a *Notice of Levy* for $134,900. The tax was computed on the full $580,000 selling price of his home. The IRS closed his bank account and seized his meager retirement savings. At this point, he had a *negative* net worth; he was flat-out reduced to pauperism. In the end, the IRS settled for $30,000 on its $135,000 levy. This was a 1988 case settled in 1997.

Last "Address of Record"

Well over 50% of IRS notices sent out incur no response for one simple reason. They are mailed to an old address. It has been a long established policy that one's "address of record" is that which appears in the address block on the latest tax return filed. That address is certified correct by signing the return "under penalties of perjury" that—

[All] *accompanying schedules and statements . . . are true, correct, and complete.*

In reality, there is a 3-year window within which the IRS can pick at your latest filed return. This 3-year window is set forth in Section 6501(a): *Limitations on Assessment and Collection.* It states in part—

The amount of any tax imposed . . . shall be assessed within 3 years after the return was filed (whether or not such return was filed on or after the date prescribed).

It is the address on the return being picked at to which a notice is sent. It is *not* the address on the very latest return being filed. The latest return filed is processed by a different IRS group from that which is processing the "within 3-years" return. Because of the internal complexity of IRS operations, it is administratively infeasible for the IRS to completely update its computer data base within every 12-month period. For this reason, various courts have ruled that a tax return on its own is *not* a "clear and concise notification of a change of address."

Suppose, for example, that you filed your 1997 return on August 15, 1998. It takes approximately 18 to 24 months for the IRS to decide whether it is going to send you a notice regarding that return. Once the decision is made, it takes another six to 12 months for the notice to actually be sent out. As long as it is mailed from an IRS office on or before August 14, 2001 (within three years), you have been properly notified. The notice is valid and enforceable. The validity holds even if the notice went to your form 1997 address, after your subsequent-year returns (1998, 1999, and 2000) showed a different address. The "within 3-year" address of record stands as a legal notice.

As is always the case with IRS notices, the burden is on the taxpayer to inform the IRS of any change in pertinent information. This burden is particularly crucial in the case of joint returns. Section 6212(b)(2): *Address for Notice of Deficiency,* says—

*In the case of a joint return filed by husband and wife, [any] notice of deficiency may be a single joint notice, **except that if the** [IRS] **has been notified by either spouse** that separate residences have been established, then, in lieu of the single joint* *notice, a duplicate of the original joint notice shall be sent . . . to each spouse at his last known address.* [Emphasis added.]

In the AFL and HEB cases above, none of the four spouses notified the IRS of the different addresses. The consequences, as we've seen, were devastating to the two husbands. Obviously, the address-of-record problem is one that seems destined to never end. Free people must always be free to move around.

Should Use Form 8822

Over the years, one's address of record, or "last known address" as the IRS refers to it, has been a highly litigious issue. By mailing tax and penalty demands to an old address, billions of dollars of revenue have been hijacked from taxpayers and pumped disreputably into the U.S. Treasury. Various courts, more sympathetic to the IRS than to taxpayers, have held that the latest return filed does not provide sufficient notice to the IRS of a change of address. Internal processing time and the within-3-year rule (Section 6501(a) were impediments.

A turning point occurred in 1988 with the case of *Abeles v. IRS* [91 T.C. 1019]. The *Abeles* court held that the most recently filed and properly processed return was one's last known address, **unless the IRS has been given clear and concise notification** of a different address. The term "properly processed" was not defined by the court. This was left up to the IRS.

Subsequent to the *Abeles* case, on March 26, 1990, the IRS published **Revenue Procedure 90-18** [1990-1 CB 491]: *Procedures for Change of Address.* Procedure 5.04(1) requires that a clear and concise written notification be sent by any taxpayer who has changed address since filing his latest return. For this purpose, **Form 8822**: *Change of Address*, is to be used. This form will be considered "properly processed" after a 45-day period which begins the day after its receipt by the IRS processing center for the old address.

In addition to the old address, the form must contain each taxpayer's full name, social security number, and new address. Separate spousal lines are provided for—

Husband: Name —   old address —   new address
Wife: Name —   old address —   new address

Instructions on the back of the form say—

*If you or your spouse changed your name due to marriage, divorce, etc. complete the **Prior name(s)** line. Also, be sure to notify the Social Security Administration of your new name.*

Procedure 4.06 makes it clear that—

A taxpayer should notify the U.S. Postal Service facility serving [his] *old address of* [his] *new address. However,* [such] *notification **does not constitute** the clear and concise written notification required* [by] *the IRS.*

In all cases, Form 8822 must be filed with the IRS Center serving your *old address*. We stress this procedural point in Figure 2.2. If you inadvertently send it to the IRS Center for your new address, you become a high-stakes roulette player. To the new center, you are a new account which hasn't filed a tax return. Computer demands for all past tax returns will gush forth. It is the old center, not the new, that has your tax history in its data base. It is the old center that will keep pumping out notices and demands until you respond.

Form 8822 should be filed separately on its own. Do not include it as an attachment to some other form, schedule, or statement that you may be sending to the old IRS Center. Make Form 8822 a stand-alone document. Send it by CERTIFIED MAIL — RETURN RECEIPT. The returned receipt will indicate the official date that starts the 45-day processing period mentioned above. You need take no further action until the IRS contacts you.

Before Responding: Peruse

Not every IRS notice is a demand for more money. Many contacts are purely procedural, correctional, or informational in nature. Maybe an entry on your return was illegible; maybe you

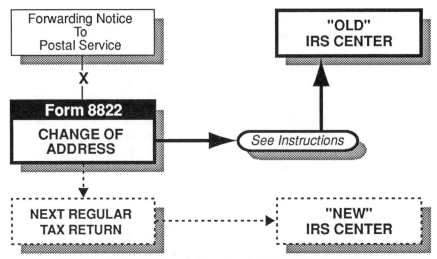

Fig. 2.2 - Where to Send Change of Address Form to IRS

entered on the wrong line; maybe you mixed up the social security numbers of your children; maybe you added or subtracted wrong; maybe you didn't claim certain credits properly; or maybe something else on your return was askew which needs to be clarified before processing can continue. Yes, some of the notices will demand more money; some may even inform you of a refund. You just don't know from the outside of an envelope.

When you open an envelope with the words *Internal Revenue Service* on the outside, do not panic. You are not going to jail. Calmly open the envelope and spread the notice out flat on a nearby table. Usually, there are two copies of the same notice: one for your records, and one for returning to the IRS when responding. Separate the two copies and handmark them No. 1 and No. 2. Set the No. 2 copy (IRS's) aside, and concentrate solely on copy No. 1.

Before you think about responding, peruse the notice carefully. Study its layout, its number of pages, and identify its computations. Look first in the upper right-hand corner. It lists such items as:

1. IRS document and processing number
2. Date of notice
3. Year or period of return
4. Tax form number

5. Your Tax ID number

Verify your Tax ID, your name, and your latest correct address. You want to make sure that you are indeed the addressee intended.

Next, *skim* the main body of the communication to see if it makes sense. Try to understand it, but don't get too engrossed in details. You just want to know, generally, what the IRS is questioning. If you can't figure out what the issue is, stop and go get the tax return or tax form referenced in the upper right-hand corner. If you can't match up the return or form with the notice you received, set the matter aside for awhile.

Look for the time allowed for any response. Somewhere on the notice — either on the front, back, or in the small print therewith — there should be some indication that you have 15, 30, or 60 days to respond. If no response time is indicated, it may be that no response is required. You may owe nothing or you may be getting a refund. We think the odds are on the side of your having to respond, to one extent or another.

Do not rush to respond prematurely. If you have 30 days to respond, for example, use 20 days to absorb and understand what the notice is about. You want to get the lay of the land, and know what you are doing. Figure 2.3 may be a helpful guideline in this regard. We call this procedure: "panic avoidance."

Phone & Log On

It would be nice if you could prepare a written response, mail it in, and be done with it. This won't work. The IRS won't wait for your written response. Its computer is preprogrammed to keep dunning you until it can legally start collection enforcement.

To stall the enforcement process, phone the IRS. Use the 800# listed in the upper right-hand portion of the notice, under the words—

For assistance, you may call us at:
1-800-_____

Below this number appears . . . *Caller ID:_____*

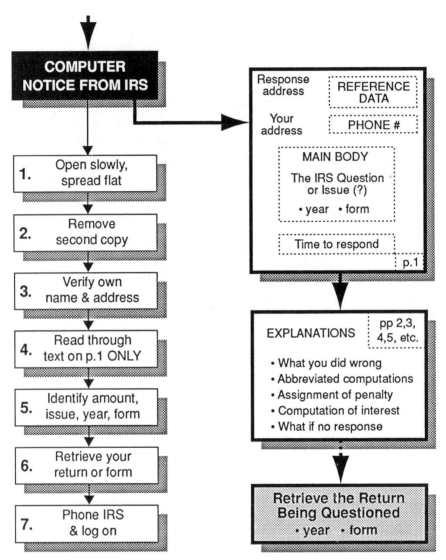

Fig. 2.3 - Panic Avoidance Technique When Opening IRS Notice

This "caller ID" is a 6-digit number assigned to the particular notice sent to you. It has no relation to your social security number (which is 9 digits) or other Tax ID; it is simply for caller identification purposes only. You may call, but you don't have to.

Our advice is that you do call. Being an 800# to the IRS, you will have trouble getting through. Your best chance, we think, is early in the morning. Try phoning at least two or three times. In anticipation of getting through, be sure to have the IRS notice in front of you, **and** the tax return or form for the at-issue year.

After the menu choices and punching in your Tax ID and Caller ID — and being put on hold — you may get a human voice. It may be a pleasant voice, a stern voice, or an arrogant voice. All answerers are trained to say: "How may I help you?" They are all there to assist you (if they can).

If there is some error in your name, address, or Tax ID, be sure to correct this on the spot. On such matters, most answerers will be accommodating because verifying such information is important not only to you but also to the IRS. If you don't understand what the notice is all about, the answerer may be able to explain what it is, or at least identify its origin on your tax return or form. DO NOT engage in any argumentative matters. All you are trying to do is find out what the issue is, and how many days you have in which to respond. If no specific response time is indicated on the notice, if requested by you, the answerer will assign a time. Typically, 20 to 30 days are given.

Before putting down your phone, specifically request that your call (date and time) be logged on the account data that is pulled up on the IRS's computer screen. Although logging on is not an acceptable response, it is indicative of your good intentions. It can save your being sent a second or third notice on the same issue.

If the issue is a "one liner" and if the answerer can display on his/her computer screen an exact duplicate of that which is on your return or form, then — perhaps — the issue can be resolved by phone. Approximately 10 percent of notice issues are resolved this way. More acceptably, your response has to be in some written form with line-by-line notations and corrections.

Here's An Example

Approximately 90 percent of notice issues require a detailed response in writing. To exemplify this need, we cite the true case of taxpayer MNF. He had a small business selling hair products wholesale from his own warehouse. His return was quite complicated; this meant that he was subject to the alternative minimum tax (AMT). Computing the AMT required the attachment of a 28-step form (namely: Form 6251) to his regular tax return (Form 1040). The year at issue was 1996.

MNF filed his 1996 return on February 28, 1997 — well ahead of the prescribed due date. On March 31, 1997 he received from the IRS a notice which read in key part—

WE CHANGED YOUR ACCOUNT — YOU HAVE AN AMOUNT DUE

As a result of this change, you owe $29,526.88. **If you think we made a mistake,** *please call us at the number listed above. When you call, please have a copy of your tax return available.*

The notice continued with 14 lines of recomputation of tax followed by an "Explanation of Penalty and Interest Charges."

MNF had already paid $57,146 to the IRS with his return. He was not about to pay another $29,500 without checking with his tax preparer. On checking MNF's Form 6251: *Alternative Minimum Tax — Individuals*, it was noted that line 17, which should have been left blank, had an entry in it. The entry amount was the sum of lines 15 and 16, which also showed up in lines 18 and 19. Lines 18 and 19 were correct. For instructional purposes, we present actual numbers in Figure 2.4. The total tax as computed on MNF's original return *was* correct. The IRS was *not* correct.

MNF phoned the designated 800# and tried to explain the situation. The IRS answerer acknowledged that line 17 (on Form 6251) was the issue, but he couldn't do anything about it over the phone. The answerer did suggest that an amended return (Form 1040X) be prepared and filed within the next 30 days. The end result was that no additional tax was due. Issue closed.

No Human IRS Eyes

The IRS has a disturbingly high error rate in its "We Changed Your Account" notices. Many errors are made because all tax

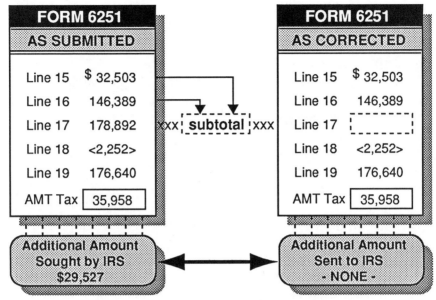

Fig. 2.4 - Example When Questioning IRS Computer Notice

returns and forms go through *automatic electronic processing*. No human IRS eyes ever look at the routinely processed returns any more. The computer does everything. Touch a key; click a mouse: returns are processed, notices go out, and revenue gushes in. What good are humans anymore?

In the MNF case above, had a set of IRS eyeballs looked at Form 6251, it would have been self-evident that line 17 was an aberration. Mental arithmetic would have revealed that it was a subtotal of lines 15 and 16 which went onto line 19. The lines 18 and 19 were correct as entered. Yes, line 17 should have been left blank (as per Figure 2.4). But it had no effect on the bottom line tax . . . except for the stupid computer.

We have another case illustrating the stupidity of computer scanners. They can't read handwritten notations and computations on a tax form.

Taxpayer REL was a 1996 retiree who received three Forms 1099-R citing his retirement income for the year. Each 1099-R form required the extraction of three entries and combining them altogether onto **Form 4972**: *Tax on Lump-Sum Distributions*.

Form 4972 is a 38-line form with about $3^1/2$ inches of blank white space at the bottom of its page 2. All the backup computations were shown here. The bottom line amount was correctly entered on the Form 1040 line designated as *Tax*. The entry was $6,710.

Associated with the Form 1040 tax line, there is a blank checkbox captioned: Form 4972. REL's preparer checked this box and hand-entered alongside of it the following notation:

☒ Form 4972. "See computations on page 2 of Form 4972."

Although no one expected the computer to scan-read the hand-printed notation, it should have been able to read the X-mark in the checkbox. It didn't. Yet, it automatically computed that REL owed another $2,226 in additional tax.

Eventually, the matter was resolved. But it took the submission of nine documents to the IRS including Form 1040X: *Amended U.S. Individual Income Tax Return*. Accompanying the nine documents, there were grammar school level instructions for "walking the IRS through" REL's response. The tax as initially entered on the return was indeed correct.

There is one consolation to having to prepare a written response to an IRS touch-of-a-key computer notice. The computer can't read the response. Therefore, human IRS eyeballs have to read it!

Electronic Looting: Unstoppable

Our guestimate is that around 20% of all tax, penalty, and interest revenue collected by the IRS is through errors in its automatic processing procedures. To put it starkly: the 20% is **electronic looting**! Most taxpayers don't seem to catch on. They are so intimidated by any computer notice from the IRS that they hurriedly pay, just to "get it over with." This looting partly explains why the national debt is being reduced more rapidly than politicians ever dreamed possible.

The IRS knows full well that its electronic looting is taking place. When it sends out a change of account notice, the pertinent issue is addressed in only about four to eight lines. The lines are all bunched together in monolithic computer typescript. Blended into this monolith is **one** of the following "we admit it" phrases:

If you think we made a mistake . . .
If you disagree with any of the changes we made . . .
If you don't agree . . .
If you have any questions . . .
If you can't pay in full . . .

Whichever "If" phrase is applicable to your notice is mentioned only once. It is intended that you miss it. To assure this, the penalty and interest phrases are mentioned over and over again, several times. The IRS uses about 100 lines to compute the penalties and interest, and warn you that they continue until the additional tax is paid. You become befuddled and totally lose track of the one "If" phrase. This is outright deception under the guise of law.

Congress has blessed electronic looting, and has already authorized the IRS to extend it. On August 20, 1996: Small Business Job Protection Act, Congress added Subsection 6302(h) to the IR Code. This subsection is titled: *Use of Electronic Fund Transfer System for Collection of Certain Taxes*. This is referred to as the EFTS tax collection process. It requires all businesses owing more than $50,000 in federal taxes (of all types) per year, to transfer the amounts from their financial accounts directly to the IRS. No bank intermediary is involved. For smaller businesses (the "protection" bit), the transfers are via TAX LINK which includes a bank intermediary. Any failure to deposit taxes electronically is subject to further penalties and interest (of course).

On August 5, 1997, in the Taxpayer Relief Act, Congress extended the TAX LINK concept to individual taxpayers. It authorized the IRS to accept payment for taxes by credit cards, debit cards, or charge cards. Former Section 6311: *Payment by Check or Money Order*, has been retitled to: *Payment of Tax by Commercially Acceptable Means*. Whereas the former Section 6311 consisted of about 200 words, the revised section consists of about 1,200 words. Additional legal words are necessary because individual electronic transfers — by TAX LINK or other — are subject to special collection enforcement procedures, should there be miscommunication between the taxpayer, his financial institution, and the remittable balance in his account. With EFTS becoming the "tax collection wave of the future," we are terrified at the prospects of abuse by the IRS. You should be terrified, too.

States Electronically Loot Also

The electronic collection wave of the future applies also to income taxing states. Delinquency information generated by the IRS is sent directly to your state taxing authority at the same time its notice is sent to you. This is by virtue of IRC Section 6103(d): *Disclosure to State Tax Officials and State and Local Law Enforcement Agencies.* In other words, the IRS has *exchange agreements* with state tax officials. It's the Big Brother–Little Brother syndrome. If you don't respond to an IRS notice, you are presumed not to have responded to a state tax notice.

A state like California — the prima donna goon state — doesn't wait until an IRS matter is resolved. The moment it gets information, it electronically files a State Tax Lien against the taxpayer and his assets. It then demands payment within 20 days. If no immediate payment, California levies and loots your monetary assets. Never mind that the IRS may be totally or partially wrong.

There is a "bizarre twist" to these IRS-state tax information exchanges. Which gets priority of tax liens? A Federal Tax Lien applies automatically if no payment within 10 days of demand [IRC Sec. 6321]. Under the Federal Tax Lien Act (P.L. 89-719), the IRS has a priority over all state and local government tax liens. But states like California ignore this priority law. We have a specific case on point.

In our HEB case on page 2-6, the IRS had seized $30,000 of HEB's IRA account, leaving $21,876 as a "tax reserve" for his 1997 taxes. Before the arrangement was completed, California preemptively seized the $21,876. This left HEB totally penniless; the IRS and California seized **all** of his assets. A similar fate could happen to *you*, in our electronic tax wonderland.

3

WHEN NO RETURN FILED

> If, For Whatever Reason, You Fail To File A Tax Return When Required, It May Take From 5 To 10 Years To Be "Overdue Notified" By The IRS. This Span Of Time Can Lead To A False Sense Of Security, And Cause Other Nonfilings To Occur. The Computer Generated Notices Make Outrageous Tax And Penalty Demands. They Are Designed To Get Attention! State Tax Agencies Also Pile On. Regardless Of One's Reason For Not Filing, A Return MUST BE FILED For Each Nonfiling Year. It Is Only AFTER Said Filing(s) — Federal And State — That You Can Disagree With The Egregious Demands Made. Meanwhile, Collection Enforcement Goes On.

As mentioned in the previous chapter, it is general knowledge that individuals and entities generating income in excess of prescribed exemption amounts must file a tax return. It is also general knowledge that when a return is filed, the IRS must begin its assessment and collection procedures within three years of the filing date.

What is not general knowledge is what happens when no return is filed. When there is no return — or no acceptable return — the three-year rule does NOT apply. This means that it is "open season" for the IRS to do whatever it wants, whenever it wants. No statute of limitations applies.

Basically, what the IRS does is to prepare a return on your behalf using informant information reported to it. It does this for the sole purpose of assessing maximum possible tax, penalties, interest, and other additions. Such a "return" is NOT a substitute for your filing a return. An IRS-prepared return is legal authority for the IRS to chase a nonfiler down and sweat him out. We'll certainly describe this process for you in this chapter.

Included in the context of no returns are substitute returns, incomplete returns, false returns, protester returns, and fraudulent returns. The point is that, until an acceptable return is filed by the taxpayer and signed "under penalties of perjury," no disagreement rights exist whatsoever. One cannot disagree with his duty to file a return, if he is otherwise required to do so. Even when legally not required to file, it is often better to do so than to experience the computer tyranny that the IRS has mastered. We'll explain all of these matters herein.

All no return cases carry special penalties of their own. We'll not go into the no return penalty issues. The primary focus in this book is on disagreeing with the IRS on its assertion of the correct tax. Penalties, interest, and other additions derive directly from the correct amount of tax due and unpaid. When you disagree and reduce the tax, you automatically reduce the add-ons.

No Statute of Limitations

The 3-year rule of general knowledge is referred to as the "Statute of Limitations." It gets this designation from Section 6501: *Limitations on Assessment and Collection*. If there were no limitations on IRS power, this country long ago would have become a tax dictatorship. We attribute the absence of such state of affairs to bona fide return filers who disagree with the IRS when it is wrong. There, of course, has to be a limit to the limitations.

The wording of Section 6501(a): *General Rule*, pertinent to this chapter is—

> *Except as otherwise provided in this section, . . . no proceeding in court without assessment for the collection of such tax shall be begun after the expiration of . . . 3 years after the return was filed.*

Without the "except as otherwise" clause, if no return is ever filed, the IRS's hands would be tied. As a fantasy, many taxpayers would like this. Nonfiling would become the rule: not the exception. Congress, the Administration, and the federal courts would never accede to such nonfilings. Thus, enter subsection 6501(c): *Exceptions.*

Subsection 6501(c) actually lists nine exceptions to the 3-year rule. Only three of these exceptions are pertinent here. The applicable exceptions are: (1) *No return*, (2) *False return*, and (3) *Fraudulent return*. In the case of no return, the prescribed wording is—

> *In the case of failure to file any return, the tax **may be assessed**, or a proceeding in court for the collection of such tax **may be begun** without assessment, **at any time**.* [Emphasis added.]

This is saying that when a return is not filed (within the time prescribed), the IRS may assess tax and start collection enforcement procedures at any time. In this respect, the 3-year rule is null and void.

Similar wording applies to false returns (with intent to evade tax) and fraudulent returns (with willful attempt to defeat tax). False and fraudulent returns are treated as no returns. The difference from no returns is that more stringent penalties apply.

The net effect is that when no return is filed when it should have been filed, or when a false or fraudulent return is filed, the 3-year rule limiting the IRS does not apply. The IRS is granted "open season" license. The hunting season remains open until an acceptable return is filed. This could take five years, 10 years, 15 years . . . or 50 years! For practical reasons, rarely does the IRS let nonfiling matters continue for more than 10 years.

What Constitutes "No Return"

When a person or entity is required to file a return, official forms published by the IRS must be used. All IRS regulations therewith must be followed. Any "tampering" with the forms negates the document as a return. Tampering consists of disguising income sources, entering nonnumeric words or phrases in the dollar entry lines, and either rewording or striking out the jurat clause (*under penalties of perjury*) above one's signature to the return. The absence of a signature on an official form also constitutes no return, as does an intentionally illegible signature.

In a landmark case in 1984 [*Badaracco*, 464 US 386], the Supreme Court set forth a four-part test to establish a valid return. The tests were:

(1)   There must be sufficient data on the IRS forms to calculate the tax liability;
(2)   The document must purport to be a return;
(3)   There must be an honest and reasonable attempt to satisfy the requirements of law;
(4)   The taxpayer must execute the return under penalty of perjury.

By not meeting any one of these tests, the document is not a return. Thereupon, no limitations exist on how or when the IRS can begin its assessment and collection actions.

On occasions, "blank" return forms are filed. A blank return is one on which the taxpayer's name and address are shown, and only one line is used to show some minimal amount of income. All other lines are either left blank, or filled in with zeros, "none," "object," "5th amendment," or "self-incrimination." Usually the penalty of perjury statement is signed, with alterations. A blank return is obviously no return because there is insufficient data for determining the correct tax liability.

A return filed "under protest" is considered a return, if the four tests above are met. In an interesting case [*L.P. McCormick*, DC NY, 94-1 USTC ¶ 50,026], the taxpayer signed properly under the perjury clause. Under his signature he added the words: *Under protest*. The court held that these words were protected under the First Amendment: Freedom of Speech. The court reasoned that any citizen could protest to any government agency, including the IRS. Thereupon, the IRS had to accept the filing as a proper return.

Returns using constitutional arguments as a basis for not completing an official form properly are not returns. The IRS summarily rejects these returns as being protester returns. Arguments are advanced that the income tax is unconstitutional and that it violates their rights of freedom of speech, freedom of religion, right to privacy, right to due process, right against self-incrimination . . . and so on. Constitutional arguments on a tax return just don't fly. If such arguments are integrated into an official form in any manner, the return will be deemed a "no return." However if one completes a return form correctly, and attaches to it a separate statement of his constitutional, religious, or other objections, the return will be accepted. The IRS simply detaches the statement and tosses it away. Such a statement is not an official form.

The same IRS objection applies to fake returns, sham returns, fraudulent returns, "family estate" trusts, vow of poverty returns, and others which do not comply with official forms and regulations. Obviously, if no return of any kind is filed, there is no rejection on the IRS's part. Simply, no return has been filed.

"Extension" Is No Substitute

For millions of taxpayers, April 15th every year is a dreaded date. A crisis mentality emerges whereby depression, despair, and immobility set in. So common is this situation that a special tax form has been devised to relieve the crisis atmosphere that surrounds April 15th. Hence, the emergence of **Form 4868**: *Application for Automatic Extension of Time to File . . . Tax Return*. This is an automatic 4-month extension of time to file; it is NOT an automatic extension of time to pay.

Despite its official heading (Application, etc.), Form 4868 is fundamentally a *payment voucher*. The entire form is about four inches high and wide enough to fit into an ordinary business-size envelope (along with your payment check). If no payment check, Form 4868 is null and void.

The application portion on Form 4868 is a small-print one liner. It reads: "I request an automatic 4-month extension of time to August 15. . . ." The main body of the form addresses your estimated total tax liability for the year. Specifically, you are directed to enter as follows:

a. Total tax liability for the year $_____
b. Total payments already made $_____
c. **Balance due.** Subtract b from a $_____
d. **Amount you are paying** $_____

Other than your name, address, and Tax ID number(s), no signature is required. You are expected to estimate your total tax liability for the year, with a reasonable degree of good faith and care.

If a 4-month extension is not enough time to get your act together and get your return filed, you have one more chance at an additional two months. But this is your last. This time, you must have good and compelling reason. You must be able to show "severe or undue hardship" . . . and explain that hardship convincingly. There is a separate form for this purpose, namely **Form 2688**: Application for *Additional Extension* of Time to File.

A precondition to filing Form 2688 is that you have filed Form 4868 and made full payment of your estimated tax liability. Whereas Form 4868 has space for entering the amount of payment you are making, Form 2688 makes no provision for payment. Form 2688 is simply a chance for an additional two months' extension (once payment has been made).

Many persons file extension forms religiously, pay all the tax, and inwardly believe that they have filed the equivalent of a return, or at least a good substitute for it. Such is NOT THE CASE! An extension is just that: an *extension* (of time to file). It is not a substitute return whatsoever. If a regular return is not filed when the extension period expires, the "applicant" is treated as a nonfiler. Many thousands of nonfiling situations derive from this one misconception alone.

Similar, substitution-like situations arise when filing official forms, such as, for example Form W-2: Wage & Tax Statement. For many, the true income has been reported, and the appropriate tax has been withheld. Subsequently, no regular return is filed. Form W-2 is **not** a return. Nor is Form 1099-MISC: Miscellaneous Income & Tax Withheld. Nor is Form 1040ES: Estimated Tax Voucher. Nor is Form 1040-V: Payment Voucher. Nor is Form 1040X: Amended Return. The beliefs of many such filers are that they have filed on official forms, and paid all the tax. What more does the IRS want?

Answer: It wants a "proper return" for each nonfiling year. If there's been one nonfiling year 10 years ago, it wants a return for the nonfiling year. Never mind that full tax may already have been paid. If there have been 10 nonfiling years in a row, it wants 10 proper returns, also 10 years in a row. For individuals, it wants either a Form 1040, Form 1040A, Form 1040EZ, Form 1040-TEL (Telefile), 1040NR (Nonresident alien), or 1040-C (Departing alien). Until whichever of these forms is applicable is filed, all alleged substitutes are nonreturns.

We summarize most of the above for you in Figure 3.1.

Returns Executed by IRS

When no proper return has been filed, the IRS has authority to execute a return on its own. The IRS can do so using information supplied to it by payer informants. No attempt is made by the IRS to get correct information: just sufficient information on which it can assess a tax and commence collecting it. Any such return prepared by the IRS does NOT relieve the taxpayer of his obligation to file a proper return. An IRS-executed return is simply for administrative convenience only.

The authority for an IRS-executed return is Section 6020(b): *Execution of Return by Secretary* [IRS]. Here the term "Secretary" is Secretary of the Treasury, to whom the IRS reports. In all tax matters, the terms Secretary and IRS are synonymous.

Section 6020(b) consists of two paragraphs. These read essentially in full as follows:

> *(1)* *Authority to Execute Returns* — *If any person fails to make any return required by any internal revenue law or regulation . . . at the time prescribed therefor, or makes willfully or otherwise, a false or fraudulent return, the* [IRS] *shall make such return from* [its] *own knowledge as from such information as* [it] *can obtain through testimony or otherwise.*

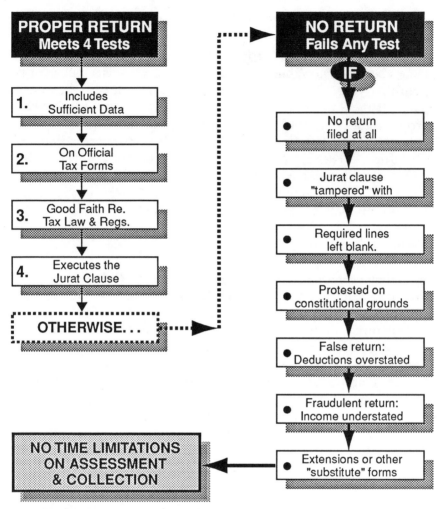

Fig. 3.1 - What Constitutes "No Return" for Enforcement Purposes

*(2)   Status of Returns — Any return so made and subscribed
by the [IRS] shall be prima facie good and sufficient for
all legal purposes.*

It is significant to know that an IRS-executed return carries no
signature, nor is it prepared "Under penalties of perjury." Cynically,
it is an outright phony. Constructively, it is the only way the IRS

can carry out its duty. The assessed tax is outrageous and the IRS knows it is. It is intended primarily to get a nonfiler's attention. It is not until the three-clawed collection dragon (lien, levy, and seizure) breathes hot that nonfilers get the message: they must file a proper return. To comply, they must knuckle down, dig up records, and prepare it in good faith. When accepted, the IRS return is set aside.

How IRS "Returns" Used

Actually, the IRS doesn't really generate a tax return in the ordinary sense. Its so-called "return" is an entry in the electronic files that it keeps on every person with a Tax ID number assigned. It creates the amount of tax liability out of thin air, then assigns "statutory additions." When its tracking computer picks up a matching address that is current, an Overdue Notice automatically goes out.

As always, we like to cite true taxpayer cases. This time, it is the case of WFA: formerly a mortgage broker who became incurably sick. She last worked in 1984. Although she had a proper return prepared for that year, showing only $47 due, she was too sick to mail it. Because of moving around seeking medical care, she didn't hear from the IRS for many years.

One day, out of the blue — on July 17, 1997 to be exact — she received from the IRS a NOTICE OF OVERDUE TAX RETURNS. The overdue returns were identified as follows:

Year	Tax Liability	Statutory Additions	Total Due
1984	$ 507	$ 792	$ 1,299
1987	70,186	3,141	73,327
1988	7,873	382	8,255
1989	42,070	1,985	44,055
1990	8,559	447	9,006
1992	32,155	1,626	33,781
1993	27,015	1,397	28,412
[7 returns]	TOTAL AMOUNT DUE		$198,135

The notice went on to say—

*We have no record that you have responded to our previous notices. As a result, your account has been assigned to this office for enforcement action. This could include seizing your wages or property. It is important, therefore, that we hear from you **within 10 days**.*

IF YOU AREN'T ABLE TO PAY YOUR OVERDUE AMOUNT IN FULL, please call the telephone number above. Be ready to tell us what your monthly income and expenses are so we can help you arrange a payment plan.

/s/   IRS
Chief, Automated
Collection Branch

There was no way in the world that WFA, an unemployed sick woman, could prepare and file seven tax returns and simultaneously pay $198,135 in 10 days. She dutifully phoned the 800 number cited in the IRS notice.

The very next day (July 18, 1997), she wrote back to the Chief, Automated Collection Branch as follows:

I called your 800 number this morning and after waiting some 20-25 minutes finally got through to a Mr. _____. I tried to explain my situation to him, and even after I requested that he stop insulting me, he continued to be rude, abusive, and sarcastic. He graciously "gave me" 2 weeks to produce my '94, '95, and '96 returns, in addition to the 7 returns required by your letter. These demands are impossible to meet. I am currently partially disabled and totally unemployed.

/s/   WFA
Unemployed Taxpayer

Yes, the IRS notice and demand for $198,135 certainly got WFA's attention. But she was unable to explain her medical problems, that the years 1987 through 1990 were her ex-husband's income (she was recovering from three major surgeries during those years), that in 1992 she was in a near-fatal auto accident, that she did work most of 1992 and owes about $3,000 in tax (NOT the $33,781 assessed) but owes nothing for years 1993 through 1996 because of being unemployed and recuperating from the '92 accident. She had medical records, police reports, and divorce papers to support her odyssey.

How do you explain this kind of situation to an IRS collection enforcer, who sits solidly in front of a computer screen, touching a key or clicker now and then?

There is only one way. WFA **has to file** a tax return for each of those nonfiling years the IRS has questioned. No matter that the collection enforcer may be rude, abusive, or sarcastic. As a nonfiler, WFA has no disagreeing rights until all returns are in!

Engage a Tax Professional

There is no way that an ordinary taxpayer can prepare 10 separate years of tax returns and file them in 10 days' time. Not even tax professionals can do this. Records have to be dug up; memories have to be refreshed; and the rationale for late filing has to be resurrected. All back year tax forms, and back year tax rate tables and regulations have to be procured. In a situation like that of WFA above, there is no alternative but to engage a tax professional.

In fact, the IRS itself encourages the use of tax professionals. In WFA's case, the last paragraph of the overdue notice read:

IF YOU WOULD LIKE SOMEONE ELSE to call us for you, we must have a signed statement from you allowing us to disclose your tax information to such person. You should make your statement on **Form 2848: Power of Attorney and Declaration of Representative.** *You can get this form from any IRS office. You must send us a copy of the completed form before your representative calls.*

IRS power of attorney form is a 2-page preprinted document limited strictly to tax matters. On page 1, the taxpayer names and identifies his appointed representative, the extent of authority the representative has, and the tax issues, forms, and years involved. Page 2 of the form requires signature of the taxpayer, followed by an "Under penalties of perjury" declaration by the representative. The declaration attests to the representative's professional qualifications, license authority, and relationship (if any) to the appointing taxpayer.

There is one outstanding advantage to engaging a professional tax return preparer (TRP). The appointee becomes an emotion-saving *intermediary* between the IRS and a distraught taxpayer. As depicted in Figure 3.2, a TRP can act as a screening and filtering agent. Said intermediary can screen information that you are willing to provide to the IRS, to prevent you from providing more than you need to provide. He also can provide screening against the IRS when it overreaches and intimidates beyond that for which it is authorized.

There is also another comforting feature with TRPs. They must exercise *due diligence* with respect to:

(a) The accuracy of all information submitted to the IRS, as required by law;
(b) The correctness of any oral or written representations made either to the appointee or to the IRS; and
(c) The promptness of submission to the IRS of lawfully requested documents and records that support the information on a return.

Once Form 2848 is authenticated, your TRP can make a phone call to the IRS and request some "breathing time." Usually, from 30 to 60 additional days can be allowed. Modest reprieves from the 10-day demands are almost always granted to professional representatives.

Prepare "Zero Tax" Year(s) First

Once you get a reprieve from the 10-day demands of the IRS, you can sit down and think through a preparation schedule and strategy. One can't do this intelligently when being threatened with

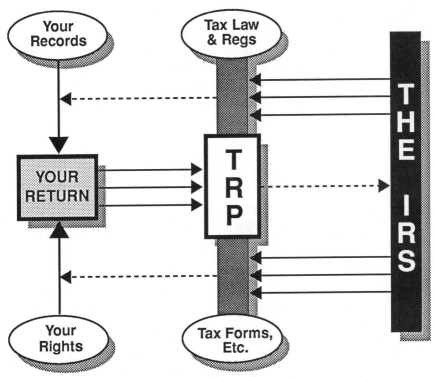

Fig. 3.2 - The Screening / Filtering Role of Tax Professionals

penalties and grossly erroneous demands. A reprieve is not forgiveness. It is only to allow you time to demonstrate good faith in filing your nonfiled returns.

When there are multiple years of returns to be filed, the problem is where to start. Where are the records and where are the tax forms you need? Do you start at the farthest back year and work forward? Or, do you start at the latest year and work backward? Or, do you start in the middle and work backward and forward? Much depends on the facts and circumstances of each nonfiler's case. It also depends on the number of nonfiling years. If the number is three or less, file them in sequential order. If more than three nonfiling years, adopt a "strategy."

Over multiple years of nonfilings, there is likelihood that one or more years may be low or no tax years. If self-employed during those years, there may be one or more business loss years. Periods of unemployment, health issues, divorce matters, and business losses can readily produce low or no tax years. These are probably the very reasons for the nonfilings. There may also be years of special problems, such as a natural disaster, murder, suicide, drug addiction, or alcoholism, where records are lost or destroyed.

In view of what we've just said, we suggest a three-pronged filing strategy. You prepare and file in following order:

I   — Zero tax years
II — Low tax years
III — Problem tax years

There is psychology and pragmatism in this three-pronged approach. By filing the "zero tax" years first (including business loss years), you soon become aware that when there is no tax, there also are no penalties, no interest, and no additions. And when you compare your zero tax with that which the IRS has assessed, you begin to realize that you are being gouged by your own government. These realizations do wonders for your psyche and strengthen your determination to file them all . . . in proper time.

Filing zero tax years includes those years that you are not required to file, by omission from the IRS's 10-day demand notice. For example, in WFA's initial notice, the year 1991 was omitted. Could it be that the IRS was not payer informed of low amounts of income? Or, did it just slip through the system? Common sense tells you that when you start filing the demanded year returns, sooner or later any return omitted from the demand notice will be questioned. In WFA's case, filing the omitted 1991 return was tax advantageous. It turned out to be an NOL (Net Operating Loss) deduction. An NOL is a business loss which can be carried back and used in years 1988, 1989, and 1990.

The NOL carryback rule is prescribed in subsection 172(b)(1)(A)(i): *Net Operating Loss Carrybacks and Carryovers*. It reads in pertinent part—

*A net operating loss for **any** taxable year, . . . shall be a net operating loss carryback to each of the 3 taxable years preceding the taxable year of such loss.*

In WFA's case, 1995 was also an NOL year. Subsection 172(b)(1)(A)(i) means that she can carry the NOL back to 1992 and then forward to 1991 and 1990.

Have we made our point?

By filing zero tax years first you may uncover some tax loss benefits which you otherwise would not have computed. There are also capital loss and passive loss carryovers which, if applicable, are tax useful. The IRS collection enforcers will never tell you about the tax offsetting benefits of loss carryovers and carrybacks. In its outrageous demands, the IRS intentionally hopes that you will miss taking advantage of your tax loss benefits.

File "Low Tax" Year(s) Next

How much tax is "low tax"? Obviously, this depends on what a taxpayer is accustomed to paying when he files his returns regularly and voluntarily. But when the IRS demands tax for nonfilings, we think 10% of the amount of tax demanded is low (relatively). That is, if for a stated nonfiling year the IRS demanded, say, $50,000 (tax, penalty, and interest), one's low tax would be $5,000 or less.

Let's bring into focus this second prong of one's backyears filing strategy. Again, we'll use the case of WFA and request that you glance back at her nonfiling years listed on page 3-9. Off the top of her head, she knew instantly that 1984 and 1992 would be low tax years. For each of these years, some major event occurred which, although she had taxable income, resulted in low tax due.

For tax year 1984, WFA had had her return professionally prepared on October 14, 1985. She had an IRS-approved 6 months' extension beyond the prescribed due date of April 15, 1985. She was overcome with chronic fatigue to the point where she didn't have enough energy to sign her return and deposit it in the mail. At that time, the amount of unpaid tax due was $47. Her employment withholdings took care of the bulk of her tax. When she received the IRS overdue notice in July 1997, she retrieved the previously prepared return, signed it, and sent it in. She did this on July 18, 1997 — some 12 years late. As the saying goes, "Better late than never, but better never late."

In 1992, WFA was self-employed earning a modest income. After deducting all applicable business expenses, **including** the NOL carryback from 1995, her net unpaid tax due was $2,982. This markedly differs from the $33,781 amount demanded by the IRS. Still and all, until one files a proper return, there can be no disagreement contesting the IRS's computer assessed amount. Her 1992 return was filed on August 25, 1997. Obviously, the filing was late . . . and no payment was made.

When filing late and/or paying late or not paying at all, some written explanation should be attached to the return. For this purpose, **Form 4571** is available. The form is titled: *Explanation for Filing Return Late or Paying Tax Late.* The formal portion is one-third of a page in length with two-thirds blank space for entering one's explanation. The key entry line thereto starts off with—

I did not file the above tax form or pay the required tax on time because . . .

When one files late with an amount of tax due, Form 4571 is one's only chance to get an IRS processor to take note of it. Any official form that is filed is noted. Unofficial statements attached to a return generally are ignored. In nonfiling cases, Form 4571 can be a safety net.

Again, for true case illustration purposes, WFA's Form 4571 for 1992 read as—

*I was in a car accident on 11-12-92 and suffered severe lacerations to my head (10 internal stitches; 25 external stitches), with concussion and chronic pain in my neck and back. **See photo attached.** Was hospitalized and unable to work for 8 months. Had to spend all available money on medical treatment and self-support.*
Under penalties of perjury [etc.]   /s/   WFA

The "photo attached" was a stopper of its own. It showed a just-out-of-the-hospital female, with horrible lacerations to her forehead, a right eye blackened to near closure, and massive bruises of her chin, nose, and right ear. With photo documentation of this kind, even the most hardened IRS enforcers can sense that automatic computer assessment and dunning has its cruel and inhumane side.

Do "Problem Return(s)" Last

What's a "problem return"? We'll cite an example. Also, we refer you to Figure 3.3 for strategy overview purposes.

You receive notice from the IRS that your 1987 return is overdue: you owe $73,327. You were a housewife in that year with no separate income of your own. You have no knowledge of your now ex-husband's income, and don't really know whether he filed a tax return for 1987 or not. After receiving the IRS notice, you tried to locate your ex-husband . . . to no avail. You search vainly among your papers and things, but no 1987 income records can be found. Still, the IRS wants from you $73,327. The 1987 return presents a "problem"; would you not agree? A really tough problem, yes?

In WFA's case above, she had four problem years in a row: 1987 through 1990 (she was divorced in 1991). She never worked in those years; her husband supported her entirely. He was self-employed as a building contractor. She cannot recall ever signing a joint tax return with him. Yet, the IRS is demanding from her a total of $134,643 in tax and penalties for 1987 through 1990. She HAS TO FILE a tax return for each of those years. What can she possibly do?

First off, she has to file separately from her ex-husband. She cannot file a joint return, even if she could establish his net business income. A joint return has to be signed by both spouses. If an ex-spouse cannot be located, the late filing spouse must X-mark the filing status box:

[x] *Married filing separate return*

She X's this same box for each of the four years that have not been filed.

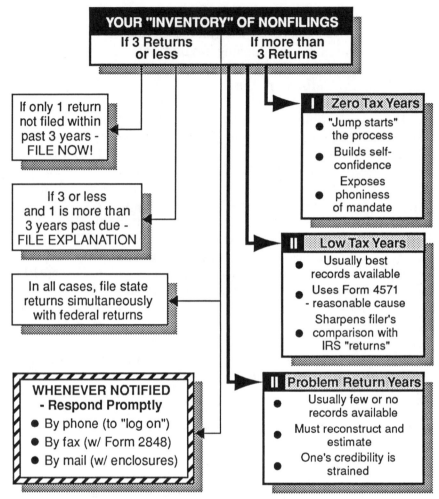

Fig. 3.3 - Strategy When "Mandated" to File Back Year Returns

Next, not knowing — and not being able to find out — what her ex-husband's income was, she has to estimate her income based on the cost of her support for each of the four years. That is, she has to estimate (with specific computations) the cost of her one-half of household rent, utilities, food, furnishings, and transportation. She enters this estimated amount for her own support as *Other income* on page 1 of Form 1040. At this line entry, there is a preprinted instruction which reads:

Other income. List type and amount.

_____ $_____

In WFA's case, she entered each year's income as:

Estimated spousal support. See attached. <u>*$12,000*</u>

The attachment was a breakdown of WFA's best estimate of rent, utilities, food, furnishings, and transportation for 1987, 1998, 1989, and 1990. She made no other entry on each return other than claiming the standard deduction and one personal exemption. The resulting tax for each year was approximately $1,000. To the front of each return she attached Form 4571 citing briefly the circumstances of her predicament.

Although the IRS claimed WFA owed a total of $134,643 for the four nonfiling years, her late filings showed a total base tax (no additions) of $4,346. She carefully read the jurat clause (under penalties of perjury) above her signature. She read aloud her affirmation that—

*I declare that I have examined this return and accompanying schedules and statements and **to the best of my knowledge and belief**, they are true, correct, and complete.*

<u>/s/   WFA   </u>

This is the best that WFA or anyone else under similar circumstances could do. The mere fact that she filed the returns in good faith puts her in a position to disagree wholeheartedly with the egregious demands ($134,643) of the IRS.

Also, File State Returns

As you prepare your backyear returns and file them with the IRS, file also the corresponding years with your state income tax authority. Most taxing states recognize the priority of filing federal returns before filing corresponding state returns. This is because, through federal-state "exchange agreements," all taxing states today piggyback the federal return. That is, each state income tax return starts with *either* the adjusted gross income or the taxable income shown on the federal return. Adjustments thereafter are made to the federal entries pursuant to each state's tax law differences.

California is different. It is a rogue state that considers itself to be a separate sovereign nation of the world. Before one can respond, it immediately files (electronically) a Notice of Tax Lien in the county where the taxpayer resides.

In WFA's case, the formal wording of a California overdue returns notice read (in part)—

The Franchise Tax Board has received a federal report showing adjustments to your federal return(s) for the year(s) shown above. Because many federal and state tax laws are the same, we review the California tax return when an adjustment is made on the federal return. [However], we are unable to locate your state return(s) for the above year(s). . . . Please provide substantiation [of your federal filings]. Reply within 20 days.

In response, WFA wrote to California's Franchise Tax Board saying (in part)—

I continue to dispute the figures shown on the IRS statement, and will dispute any corresponding figures the Franchise Tax Board may allege. . . . As I stated in my letter to the IRS (copy enclosed), my health continues to be a serious problem. I very much want to comply with both the IRS and the FTB to the degree that I am able. . . . I will complete the California returns as soon as I complete the federal returns, and copies will be sent to you.

/s/   WFA

There's a moral here, of course. If you generate any income at all, whether bottom-line taxable or not, file a return: federal **and** state. File even when you may not have to. If filing late, try to do so before ever receiving an overdue return notice. As despicable as tax enforcement procedures are, they are, nevertheless, "legal."

4

COMPUTER MISMATCHINGS

The IRS's CORNERSTONE OF THE FUTURE Is Its CP-2000 Program (Computer Matching). This Genie Relies On Payer/Informants Reporting Electronically With "Information Returns" Such As W-2s, 1099s, K-1s, Etc. Electronic Big Brothering Creates New Taxpayer Problems (On Form 1040) For Nominees, Rollovers, And Bunching Of Income And Deductions. Every Mismatching Notice Proposes An INCREASE IN TAX, Plus Penalty, Plus Interest. If You Respond Within 30 Days, You Have Three Options: "A" Agree And Pay, "B" Partially Agree And Partially Pay, Or "C" Disagree And Not Pay. If "B" Or "C," You Must Have Convincing Explanations.

Today, virtually every payer-payee transaction involving money, barter, property, services, or money-equivalent is payer-reported to the IRS. These reportings are called *information returns*. These returns cover not only salaries, wages, bonuses, commissions, tips, and nonemployee compensation, but also every conceivable transactional exchange. Included on these informational returns are interest and dividends, stock and bond sales, mutual fund redemptions and rollovers, real estate sales and exchanges, bankruptcies and debt forgiveness, gambling winnings, prizes and awards, insurance proceeds, pensions and annuities, rents and royalties, partnership income, estate and trust income, farm income, unemployment compensation, social security benefits, divorce settlements, mortgage interest . . . ad infinitum.

There are nearly 2,000,000,000 (2 billion) of these information returns filed each year. They are filed electronically through more than 50 different reporting forms. Passive payments, such as interest and dividends, as low as $10 are reported. Personal service payments of $600 or more are reported. Gambling winnings of $1,200 or more are reported. Direct sales of $5,000 or more are reported. Cash transactions of $10,000 or more are reported. Talk about Big Brother, this is it!

What do you suppose the IRS does with all of this informant reporting?

It matches all reported information with that which you, as an individual taxpayer report on your Form 1040 and its attachments. You dare not misreport, underreport, or not report the exact dollar amount attributed to you by each of your payer/informants. For if you do, the COMPUTER MATCHING WRATH of the IRS clamps down hard, demanding additional tax.

Unfortunately, in this electronic era of tax utopia, "computer errors" are made. They are made by the informants; they are made by the IRS; and they may even be made by you. So, in this chapter, we want to focus on the computer mismatching problems that occur, and how you deal with them. You must deal with them intelligently or you will lose your sanity.

The Overall Scheme

Many taxpayers do not yet realize that they are money-locked into a computer tax trap. The lock-in is irreversible. It will get tighter in the 1990s and will be total-perfect by the year 2005. Dollar information reporting is the ULTIMATE CORNERSTONE of IRS tax policy.

The IRS visualizes a paperless, humanless, fully automatic (electronic) tax system. Such a system is structured entirely around its computer-matching programs. The determination and collection processes are offshoots from its computer-matching efforts. Consequently, we think it is important that you understand the general scheme involved.

We present in Figure 4.1 our depiction of the overall matching operation. Of course, the depiction is oversimplified. But it gives you the idea of what is involved. The more payer/informants you have, and the more payer-payee transactions that you do, the more complex the computer tracking and matching become.

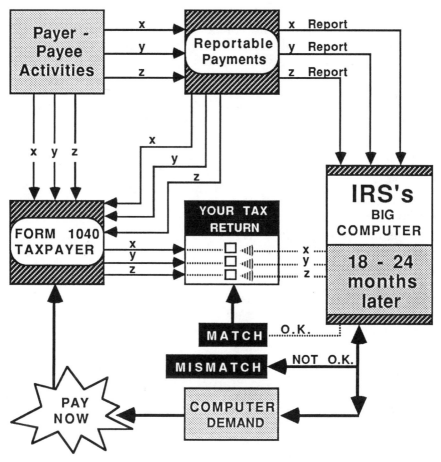

Fig.4.1 - The General Scheme of IRS's "Computer Matching"

It is significant to note in Figure 4.1 that it takes, on average, about 18 to 24 months for the IRS matching to catch up with you. This is the time lag between the due date of your Form 1040 return and the mismatching notice (computer printout) that you receive. During this interim, your attention will be on other matters and your memory of specific dollar amounts will have lapsed.

Every payer/informant who reports to the IRS on you also is supposed to send to you a paper document (either a tax form or substitute) with the same information. Many payers screw up on this. They dutifully file electronically with the IRS, or face an IRS penalty if they don't. They assume that you already know the information they are required to report, or else that it is available to you in other routine statements given to you during the year.

In Figure 4.1, we indicate that the payer is supposed to report to you at the same time he reports to the IRS. Generally, you are supposed to get the notification by January 31, but in no event later than April 15. If you don't receive any such notice, there's really not much you can do about it. You can't assess a penalty against the payer, the way the IRS can. All you can do is call the payer, reprimand him or her, or close your account there. The IRS will not accept any excuse that you did not get a copy of the payer's electronic report to it. You are required to keep better track of your own affairs.

Information Returns: General

Every employed taxpayer is familiar with Form W-2: Wage and Tax Statement. It consists of numerous dollar-entry boxes for wages, tips, other compensation, fringe benefits, pension plans, medicare, and so on. There are also dollar-entry boxes for federal income tax withholding, social security tax withholding, medicare tax withholding, state income tax withholdings, and local tax withholdings (if any). If a person works for more than one employer during the year, he/she receives a separate W-2 from each employer. An employer is obviously a "payer" of money to a "payee" (the employee).

All W-2s are classified as *information returns*. There are many other types of information returns, which we'll relate to you in a moment. All such returns are just that. They provide information only; they are **not** a tax return in the computational sense. Other than the numbered boxes thereon, there are no additions, subtractions, multiplications, or tax rate schedules involved. They are not signed by anyone, the way Form 1040 is. The payers prepare the information returns and state thereon their name, address, and EIN (Employer Identification Number).

Form W-2 is the forefather and procreator of all types of information returns. Today, there are over 50 types of such returns. For instructional identity, we classify all information returns into four distinct series, namely:

I — The W-2 series
II — The 1099 series

minimize the number of official *mismatching* notices that you may receive.

Each mismatching notice is upsetting. It is upsetting because you know that no IRS human checks the computer printouts for accuracy, nor do any human eyeballs at the IRS make any comparisons with your actual return as filed. The IRS simply sits back and lets you do all the human-matching work.

In a step-by-step sequence, we suggest the following:

Step 1 — Collect all informational returns into a *separate* workpaper file. Go through each return and highlight the form number and year. Review "substitute" forms and likewise highlight. Group all identical form numbers together.

Step 2 — Go through all W-2 series forms and highlight the *income tax* withholdings; these are your prepayments of tax. Do not confuse with social security and medicare tax withholdings.

Step 3 — Go through all 1099-series forms and highlight the *reportable payments*. Also highlight the income tax withholdings (if any).

Step 4 — Examine page 1 of Form 1040, and identify those income lines which **do not specify** the attachment of a separate schedule. For these lines only, you can group into one entry all applicable information from the payer forms.

Step 5 — Identify on page 1 of Form 1040 those lines which *do specify* the attachment of a separate schedule. On these separate schedules, for **each** information return, make **one entry** only. DO NOT GROUP the payer reportings of like form numbers. This is the greatest single cause of the genie mismatchings.

Step 6 — Unless an information return shows some income tax withholdings, do not attach it to your Form 1040. The computer already has the information it needs. For those informational forms with withholdings, make sure you retain copies for your own records.

Step 7 — Don't be foolish and try to play games with the IRS's computer-matching programs. In general, it has three years to match up your reportings with those of your payers. In certain cases, its matching time is open ended.

Step 8 — Don't expect the IRS's computer genie to pay you refunds. If you have overreported your reportable payments; if you have underreported your losses and credits; or, if you have overlooked claiming any of the withholdings, don't expect refunds. The sole purpose of computer matching is to collect maximum revenue: NOT TO PAY REFUNDS!

There is a very important message in Step 8. Under no circumstances rely on the IRS's computer matching to pick up anything on the information reporting that is in your favor. That's *your* job. The IRS's job is to pick up anything and everything in **its favor**. Once you understand this, you'll pay more attention to the growing deluge of information returns (and their substitutes).

The Nominee Problem

For computer-matching purposes, a "nominee" is another person (other than a spouse) with whom you share some part of the reportable payments. You may share such payments with one, two, or more nominee persons. However, if there is more than one owner of an account, the payer/informant is required to report only in the name of *one person* whose SSN is on the account. This creates a taxpaying problem when there are multiple owners of an account.

For example, you, your brother (or sister), and a friend co-own a brokerage account which pays out $9,000 during the year. Your agreed ownership interests are: Nominee A (yourself) 35%, Nominee B 35%, and Nominee C 30%. The payer, the XYZ Corporation, issues Form 1099-DIV showing the full $9,000 in your name (Nominee A) and SSN. How do you report the information on your Form 1040 tax return?

The proper amount of your ownership interest is $3,150 [$9,000 x 35%]. If you report this amount, what does the IRS computer see? It sees a $5,850 mismatch [$9,000 - 3,150]. It will send you a computer demand for the tax on the $5,850. And, naturally, it will add penalties and interest.

The correct way to report on your return is as follows:

XYZ Corporation (payer)	$9,000
Nominee B (name and SSN)	<3,150>
Nominee C (name and SSN)	<u><2,700></u>
	$3,150

The IRS computer picks up the $9,000 which cross-matches with the same figure the payer reported. The computer is happy. You only pay tax on the $3,150 instead of the $9,000, which should make you happy. Whether the IRS computer picks up the Nominees B and C information from your return, or whether Nominees B and C properly report on their own return, is NOT YOUR PROBLEM.

The same general procedure as above applies to all *income* schedules which attach to your Form 1040. In those cases where the attached schedules are not adaptable to the procedure above, you become a *re-issuing* payer. That is, you prepare one Form 1099-MISC for Nominee B and a separate Form 1099-MISC for Nominee C. You, yourself, then send these to the IRS using the prescribed transmittal form, namely: Form 1096 (Transmittal of Information Returns).

Reportable Deductions?

The IRS's computer-matching drive focuses primarily on payer information. This provides it the greatest opportunity for increasing your tax. But, because certain deductions can dominate a return to reduce its tax, the matching effort also includes certain large deductible items. The most common of these large deductions is mortgage interest paid.

All financial institutions who regularly lend money to borrowers must report annually the total mortgage interest paid to them. This is done on **Form 1098:** *Mortgage Interest Statement.* Instead of payer-payee, the words used on this form are: lender-borrower. It is the borrower who can claim the mortgage interest expense deduction. The 1098 information is called a *reportable deduction.*

DISAGREEING WITH THE IRS

Suppose, now, there are several co-borrowers who are co-liable for the same mortgage indebtedness. For example, suppose you co-own a parcel of rental real estate with the same persons as in the nominee example above, with the same percentage of ownership interests, namely: 35/35/30. At the end of the year, the mortgage company sends you Form 1098 showing $10,000 in your name and SSN. Now what?

If you report and claim the full $10,000 as a deduction, the IRS computer won't know the difference. But if owner/borrowers B and C report and claim their proper deduction, they will catch flak from the IRS. There is no Form 1098 information in the genie brain to match the mortgage interest deduction that B and C claim. Consequently, they have a problem. In this case, it is up to *you* to help them out.

Here's what you do. Take the Form 1098 or its substitute, which the mortgage company sent to you. In the available white space where the dollar amount of mortgage interest is shown, type (or hand print) the following:

Borrower A (your percentage: 35%)
Borrower B (name and SSN: 35%)
Borrower C (name and SSN: 30%)

Photocopy and send to B and C with instructions to attach your marked-up Form 1098 to their returns. At the line where they claim their proper share, instruct them to add the notation: "See attached."

Then you report on your return only your proper share, namely: $3,500 [$10,000 x 35%]. The computer has a $10,000 deduction in your name and SSN. When it cross-matches and finds that you are claiming less than $10,000, it is happy. The IRS is always happy when you claim any amount less than the reportable deduction. Borrowers B and C may still encounter mismatching flak, but that's now their problem. It is no longer yours.

Genie Notice: Page 1

If there is a computer mismatch between what you report on your return and that which your informant reports to the IRS, you will receive an official *mismatching notice*. It will be a computer printout with no salutation and no IRS signature. About three inches down from the top of the cover page, (namely, page 1), this heading will appear:

Notice of Proposed Change to 19 ____ Tax Return
(This is not a bill but requires a response.)

To help you orient yourself better as to what the notice contains, we present its general format in Figure 4.3. Shown there is just page 1. There are four other pages that we'll tell you about shortly.

For instructional focus, we have emphasized the heading with bold type. It does not appear this way on the notice that you will receive. On the actual IRS printout, all of the heading and subheading lettering is uniformly capitalized. There is no typographical variation in type font or density. The heading and all paragraphical contents look exactly the same. You have to read the entire 420 capitalized words on page 1 to figure out what the computer is printing out. To help you get a handle on the contents of page 1, we have numbered each paragraph in Figure 4.3 and have assigned captions of our own.

The fact that the mismatching notice comes to you in a window-type envelope, with *Department of Treasury, Internal Revenue Service* in bold type thereon, doesn't help much. As you fumble your way through the notice, you may trip across the first line in the third paragraph which reads: *within 30 days of this notice.* This is your tip-off that you've got to do something.

As we've tried to highlight in Figure 4.3, paragraph 1 describes the computer-matching process, and paragraph 2 tells you how to respond to paragraph 1. Paragraph 3 tells you that if you don't respond within 30 days, paragraph 2 becomes invalid. The proposed *tax increase* and penalties become final. You either pay in full or go into Tax Court to protest the changes.

Do note in Figure 4.3 the upper right-hand corner. It lists the date of the notice and the tax form and year of the mismatching. Don't let the 30 days from this date slip by without responding.

Note also in Figure 4.3 the lower right-hand corner. Do you see the code symbols "CP-2000"? This is the IRS's designation of its computer mismatching notice. The "CP" means Computer Program. The "2000"? Well, it's symbolic perhaps. Could it be that, by the year 2000 (or 2005), Big Brother's electronic matching is targeted to be ingeniously perfect in every respect?

We don't know about you. Many taxpayers are getting sick and tired of electronic Big Brothering our every financial transaction. To make matters worse, no IRS human eyeballs ever check the accuracy of the mismatching notices. The IRS checks your accuracy, but not its own.

	Date of Notice: _____
	Your SSN: _____
	Tax Form: _____
	Tax Year: _____

Your SSN
Your Name
Your Address

NOTICE OF PROPOSED CHANGES TO _____ RETURN

[1] **Explanation of Computer Matching.**
We are unable to locate on your return the items listed on page _____ . Please explain ....

[2] **Instructions for Response.**
Check : Box A - Full Agreement
Box B - Partial Agreement
Box C - Total Disagreement

[3] **Warning If No Response.**
After 30 Days, Notice of Deficiency; then Tax Court.

[4] **Instructions for Partial payments.**
Interest is charged until fully paid.

[5] **Instruction Sheet for Detailed Responses.**

[6] **Keep This Notice for Your Records.**

Page 1   **CP - 2000**

Fig.4.3 - Format/Contents of a Mismatching Notice, Page 1

Genie Pages 2 to 5

The "routine" notice consists of five pages. This standard length addresses up to ten mismatched items. If there are more than ten mismatched items on your return, additional computer pages are added. Each of the five pages has a definite heading and purpose. We have already commented on page 1; it is the cover page.

Page 2 is headed: ***Proposed Changes to 19 ___ I n c o m e Tax***. It then goes on to summarize the items changed, such as—

	Shown on Return	**Reported to IRS**	**Increase \<Decrease\>**
• Wages & tips	$_____	$_____	$_____
• Nonemployee comp.	_____	_____	_____
• Interest & dividends	_____	_____	_____
• Capital gains	_____	_____	_____
• Rents & royalties	_____	_____	_____
Etc.			
		Total Increase	$_____

Following this summation of the entry changes, page 2 provides a 15-line computation of the increase in tax. It shows the net tax increase, the penalty additions to tax, and the statutory interest.

Then line 15 says—

Proposed Amount Due IRS $_____

Page 3 is headed: ***Amounts Reported to IRS But Not Identified, Fully Reported, or Correctly Deducted on Your Income Tax Return for 19 ___***. Then there is a numerical listing of the mismatchings, item by item, payer/informant by payer/informant, account number by account number, the reporting form number, the attributable SSN (husband or wife, separately), the gross dollar amount reported, and the tax withholdings. With this kind of detail, you are expected to respond with comparable detail, where you disagree.

Page 4 is headed: ***Explanation of Changes***. The official explanations are rather stereotyped and do not add much to your knowledge or response rights. However, you should read carefully the paragraphs on the penalty explanations. They cite IRC Section 6662(a) for the 20% penalty on the underpayment, and Sections 6621 and 6622 for interest and daily compounding on the amount of underpayment. The penalty explanation ends with the statement that—

In the following limited circumstances, you may request a waiver of the [penalties] *by providing clear and convincing evidence that:*
1. The information document is in error and you reported the correct amount;
2. The underreporting was caused by the death or illness of the taxpayer and the information return was not available to the preparer; or
3. The underreporting was caused by the destruction of your residence, place of business, or business records by civil disturbances, fire, or other casualty.
In such cases as these, you must provide a written statement of the facts, together with any supporting documents, and request that the [penalties] *be waived.*

Page 5 (last page) of the IRS notice is headed: ***Taxpayer Response to Proposed Changes to 19 _____ Income Tax.*** Then the lead-off sentence reads—

*Please complete the appropriate section below and **return the entire page** to us in the enclosed envelope. Be sure that our address shows through the window. Please indicate the amount you paid here: $_____ .* [Emphasis added.]

Following the above instruction on page 5, you are instructed to: ***Check One—***

A. [ ] Consent to tax increase.
B. [ ] Partial agreement with proposed changes.
C. [ ] Total disagreement with proposed changes.

Whichever response you check, you must X-mark it very plainly. You place page 5 on top of your response, where it serves as your cover and transmittal letter. Do be aware that the mismatching notices change format from time to time.

Optional Response "A"

After carefully examining each mismatched item listed on page 3 of the genie notice, suppose you conclude that the IRS is right and that you had goofed. In this case, you really have only one choice.

It is to check the response box on page 5 at "A" — Consent to tax increase.

If you check this box, it means that you consent to *all* the changes that the IRS proposed. That is, if there are 10 items listed on page 3, you consent (admit) to all 10. If you find that one item of the 10 is in error, and you can confirm the error, do not check Response A.

The checkbox at Response A also reads as—

I consent to the immediate assessment and collection of the increase in tax and penalties shown, plus any interest due. I understand that by signing this waiver, I will not be able to contest these changes for this year in the U.S. Tax Court unless additional tax is determined to be due for this year.

/s/_____   _(date)_   /s/_____
    Your Signature   *Spouse's Signature*
                                                  (If joint return filed)

Once you sign at Response A, you should go back to page 1 and reread paragraph 4 thereof. This paragraph reads in full as—

You should respond even if you cannot calculate or pay any additional amount you owe at this time. Delay in signing and returning your response will increase the interest due on any amount you owe. Interest temporarily stops increasing for 30 days when we receive your signed response, and stops completely when you pay the total amount you owe. If we do not receive full payment of the amount which you agree you owe within 15 days, we will send you a bill.

Thus, if you sign Response A, be sure to send the page 5 in on time, whether you attach payment for the full amount due or not. By sending in page 5, you stop the running of interest for 30 days while the IRS processes its billing. Or, pay part of the amount due and wait for the final bill.

Optional Response "B"

If you find one or more of the IRS-alleged mismatched items to be in error, and you have the backup documents and facts to support your contention, then Response B is for you. That is, assuming that one or more other items are correct on the computer listing. The "B" response is: *Partial agreement* with the IRS's proposed changes.

The checkbox at Response B reads as—

I agree that changes in my income are necessary. My reasons for disagreeing with portions of this notice and supporting documentation are included with the attached signed statement. Send me a revised proposal of additional tax due, if any, based on such changes.

There's no signature space at the Response B section of page 5. This is because, before your response is accepted as valid, you must attach an explanatory statement which you (and spouse, if a joint return) must sign and date. Your response should also include your telephone number and best time for the IRS to call.

Make your explanation concise, yet complete. Attach supporting documents and reference them to the specific items with which you disagree. The best way to do this is to photocopy page 3 of the IRS notice and circle the disagreed item numbers in red. Then underscore or otherwise highlight the erroneous fact: the amount, the account, the payer/informant, the form, the SSN, or whatever. Make your explanations and document cross-referencings as self-guiding as possible. You have the opportunity now for human eyeballs at the IRS to *read* your explanation. At this stage, its electronic genie is bypassed.

After explaining the CP-2000 errors convincingly, go back to page 2 and photocopy it. Mark in red the corrected total increase with which you agree. And, correspondingly, correct in red the preprinted proposed amount due the IRS (at line 15).

Let's take an example. Suppose, on genie page 2, the total increase as originally shown is $8,919. The corrected increase to which you agree is $3,891. Cross through the $8,919 and show in red: $3,891. Then make a side notation showing the agreed fraction as—

$$\frac{3,891}{8,919} = 0.4363 = 43.63\%$$

At line 15 (CP-2000 page 2), suppose the preprinted proposed amount due the IRS is $4,712. Cross through this figure and show in red: $2,056 [$4,712 x 0.4363]. Then add a notation: *Payment herewith* (for the amount corrected).

Then send the whole works back to the IRS by U.S. Certified Mail. Don't wait for the full 30 days. Otherwise, there will be a follow-up computer demand on you "crossing in the mail."

Optional Response "C"

If the IRS's mismatching notice is totally wrong, as it often is, do not hesitate to X-mark Response "C" on page 5. This response is: *Total disagreement* with proposed changes.

The checkbox at Response C reads as—

I disagree with all the proposed changes listed in this notice. My reasons for disagreeing and supporting documentation are included with the attached signed statement.

Where there is total disagreement, you need not mark up pages 2 and 3 and return them to the IRS. The whole gamut of the alleged mismatchings is out of focus. Usually, there is a gross misinterpretation or misreading of the items on your return.

Here's a real-life example of a total disagreement. The taxpayer had a small business involving the sale, rental, storage, and maintenance of private aircraft. Let's call it: Sky High Enterprises, a fictitious name. The payer/informant reported on Form 1099-MISC the amount of $6,712 as *Rents*. The taxpayer included this amount on Schedule C (Profit or Loss from Business) along with other income amounts. The genie computer expected it to show up on Schedule E (Supplemental Income and Loss).

The taxpayer's explanation for total disagreement was (as slightly edited):

Though it might be argued that the rent payments should have been reported on Schedule E as supplemental income, it was included as part of the gross receipts on Schedule C. This was because of its inherent nature of contributing to the overall income of Sky High Enterprises. Sky High is involved in the sales, rentals, and maintenance of general aviation aircraft, together with flight instruction and charter activities. The rental income reported on Form 1099-MISC is for aircraft hangar maintenance facilities owned by Sky High.

I trust that the above explanation will serve to nullify any proposed changes to my tax return.

/s/_____

Name and Phone No.

IRS's "Acceptance" Answer

If properly prepared and forthright, there is always a chance that the IRS will accept the explanation you attached to Response "B" or "C." Although you are limited to 30 days within which to file your response, the IRS takes up to 90 days — sometimes longer — to answer your response. Particularly if it is going to accept a lesser amount than its proposed tax increase.

The sole purpose of the CP-2000 program is to *increase* tax revenues. It is not to decrease revenue nor pay refunds. Therefore, if there is partial payment ("B") or no payment ("C") attached to your response, the IRS is more apt to delay in answering you.

If there is total acceptance of your response, the IRS's answer letter is quite perfunctory. It is printed out by another computer program, namely: CP-2005.

In the Sky High total disagreement example above, the IRS's computer did answer. It accepted Sky High's explanation in full. Excerpts from the CP-2005 letter are as follows:

Thank you for furnishing more information to explain the income/deductions we recently wrote you about. We are pleased to tell you that we were able to clear up the discrepancy. . . . On the basis of this information, we have reconsidered your tax liability for the year indicated above and are accepting your return as filed. . . . Please disregard any notice of proposed changes or notice of deficiency you may have already received. Thank you for your cooperation.

Since the IRS's computer-matching programs comprise the cornerstone of its future operations, expect more genie notices rather than fewer of them.

5

AMENDING YOUR RETURNS

When An Original Return Is Filed By Its Due
Date (Including Extensions), It Can Be
Amended Any Time Up To 3 Years Thereafter.
For Doing So, Form 1040X Is Used. The "X" Is
For Recomputing The Correct Tax A Second
. . . Or Even Third, Time. You Amend To
Correct For Changes In Income, Deductions,
Exemptions, Credits, Filing Status, And Other
Matters That Come To Your Attention After The
Original Date Has Passed. You May Also
Amend For Refunds From Mismatching Notices,
Net Operating Losses, And "Discovering"
Favorable Rulings For Taxpayers Where The
IRS Has Preempted The Intent Of Congress.

A tax return, when timely filed, is not forever cast in concrete.
It can be changed — amended — any time up to three years after
filing. Changes/amendments can be made for good cause, such as
(a) discovery of error, (b) additional income, (c) additional
deductions, (d) credit oversights, (e) changes in filing status, (f)
carryback/carryforward of certain losses, (g) changes in payer
reportings, . . . and so on.

As long as the information on your amended return is not
frivolous or fraudulent, you have the right to amend it as each
occasion requires. Certainly, one change per tax year is well within
reason. Even two separate amendments (for the same tax year) are
acceptable, provided that each amendment has a stand-alone valid
reason. More than two — watch out! The IRS views frequent

amendments and multiple changes on an amendment as "playing games" with the system.

Having the right to amend your return can take the pressure off of trying to achieve 100% accuracy and completeness with your original return. If you have to depend on others for records and information before you can complete your return, you can be held hostage to someone else's indifference to your filing deadline. Knowing that you can always amend your return later, permits you to file on time, without becoming an addict of repetitive extension applications. Even a "wrong" return (inaccurate and incomplete though it may be) filed on time is "a return" for disagreeing rights purposes.

In this chapter, we want to familiarize you with the process of amending your returns — when necessary — and explain why amending is important in protecting other statutory rights which you have. In the process, we'll give a few examples and point out those conditions and limitations on what and when you can amend. If your amended return is filed within the prescribed statutory time frame, the IRS cannot ignore it.

Meaning of "The" Return

An amended return, in and of itself, is not a complete return. One's "return" is that which is required by Section 6012: *Persons Required to Make Returns of Income* and its regulations . . . on prescribed forms. This required return, when filed on or before its due date (including extensions), becomes THE return for all administrative procedural purposes. Said return becomes your *original* return for the designated taxable period. An original return is required for each calendar year in which you have tax reportable income.

To be accepted as an original return, it must be filed on or before the 15th day of April, following the close of the taxable year [Code Sec. 6072(a)]. If April 15 falls on Saturday, Sunday, or a legal holiday, Section 7503 says that the filing—

*shall be considered timely if it is performed **on the next succeeding day** which is not a Saturday, Sunday, or a legal* *holiday.* [Also], *the last day for the performance . . . shall be determined by including any **authorized** extension of time.* [Emphasis added.]

When filing your original return, be guided by Section 7502: ***Timely Mailing Treated as Timely Filing and Paying.*** The substance of this section is that if you properly address your return to the IRS, and affix the proper amount of postage, the date postmarked by the U.S. Postal Service will be deemed the date of delivery. This same "deemed delivery" rule applies to foreign government postal services. It also applies to *private* delivery services, if so "designated" by the IRS. A "designated delivery service" must mark on the cover of any return transmittal the date on which it was received for delivery [Sec. 7502(f)].

If your return is sent by U.S. certified or registered mail, the stamped postmark on your mail receipt is treated as the postmark date on the return. If you pay for a receipt which acknowledges delivery, your receipt is prima facie evidence that your return was delivered to the IRS office to which it was addressed.

If you file your original return within five days of a statutory due date (including authorized extensions), we urge that you do so via certified or registered mail. Every year, the last minute mad rush of tax return filings overwhelms the postal service and the IRS. Imprinting a postmark sometimes is missed. Often, a postmark is illegible. The IRS is not duty-bound to verify the postmark. Even those which are clearly legible and timely mailed often are incorrectly logged by the IRS receiving staff. When too close to the deadline, you have to take positive steps to protect your own interests.

The timely mailing/timely filing rule applies only to THE actual return itself. If there is a balance due on the return and full payment (in check or money order) is not included with the return, only that amount which accompanies the return is treated as timely paid.

The Role of Amending

When you file timely an original return (for a designated tax year), you make a declaration to the effect that—

I have examined this return and accompanying schedules and statements, and **to the best of my knowledge and belief,** *they are true, correct, and complete.* [Emphasis added.]

/s/_____Your signature_____   _____Date_____

What you are declaring is this: As of the date of your signature on your original return, it contained the best information that you had at that time. If, subsequently, new information or contrary information comes to your attention, you have the right — and the duty — to amend and correct that which was shown on your original return. Whether or not the amending information becomes part of your original return depends on when the amendment is made, relative to the return's due date.

If you amend your return *before* the due date (including authorized extensions) of the original return, the amending information becomes part of your original return. In this respect, you have filed a composite return: part original, part amendment. Any IRS examination, collection, or other proceeding against you does not toll until the statutory due date has passed.

An amendment to your return filed *after* the due date of your return is NOT treated as part of your original return. It is solely an amendment or supplement to a return already filed; it does not toll a limitation that has already begun to run. In this case, the IRS can exercise its own discretion whether to accept or reject, in whole or part, the amending information you have supplied. Normally, you are not informed of the IRS's action until about three months after filing an amended return.

The point that we are trying to make here is important. So much so that we depict it for you in Figure 5.1. Stated in another way, an amended return does not alter in any manner any administrative proceedings that are referenced to the due date of a required return. Such date is "cast" as depicted.

Time Limitations for Amending

As strange as it may seem, there is no IR Code section which specifically addresses amended returns. This is because the

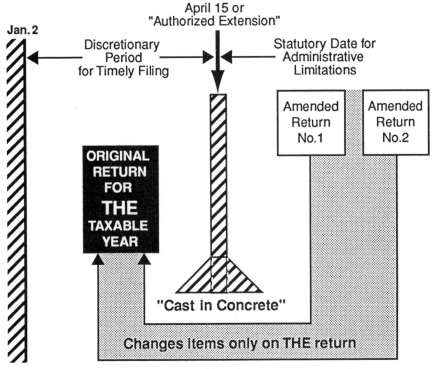

Fig. 5.1 - The "No Administrative Effect" When Amending a Return

recognition of the need for amending returns has been a long established practice of the IRS. This recognition goes back to at least 1954 when the declaration clause: "to the best of my knowledge and belief" was added to the signature portion of a required return.

Additionally, in 1954 there was an overlapping thought process involving the time limitations for claiming a credit or refund for any overpayment of tax. Up to about 1982, most amended returns were for overpayment credits or refunds. Commencing in 1982, a whole plethora of penalties was authorized for raising revenue . . . "without raising taxes." Today, nearly 25% of all Federal tax revenues are generated by the IRS assessing penalties. As a result, one of the many reasons for amending a return now is to correct and complete information which may have caused an underpayment of tax, which could bring on unwanted penalties.

Evolving from the above, we must look initially to Section 6511(a): *Period of Limitation on Filing Claim*, for the time limitations on recognizing amended returns. The portion of this section pertinent here is—

Claim for credit or refund of an overpayment of any tax imposed . . . in respect of which the taxpayer is required to file a return, shall be filed . . . within 3 years from the time the return was filed or 2 years from the time the tax was paid, whichever of such periods expires the later, or if no return was filed by the taxpayer, within 2 years from the time the tax was paid.

Thus, the general rule is within three years of the statutory due date. As explained previously, the "due date" of an individual's return is normally April 15. However, if there is an authorized extension beyond this date, the due date is that which is specified in the extension approval. Returns filed before, on, or by extension of the April 15th date are treated as timely filed. Any good faith amendment to a return within three years after its due date constitutes a valid amendment.

The two-year rule applies strictly to adjusted returns, late returns, or no returns (those prepared by the IRS), where additional tax and penalties are paid. The "date paid" means the completion of full payment. The final payment date becomes the reference date, within two years of which an amendment for a refund claim is valid. This two-year-after-payment-date is important where additional payments have been imposed by audits, administratrive processes, or judicial rulings.

Amending for Underpayments

It is pretty clear that Section 6511(a) above applies to amending returns for claiming credits or refunds when there have been overpayments of tax. But, what about amending to correct underpayments of tax?

Why would you amend a return to pay additional tax, after you have already paid what you thought was the correct tax?

Answer: The main reason is to avoid, or minimize, penalties and interest on post-return discoveries of unreported income or overclaimed deductions. The second reason is to limit the time that the IRS has for discovering, on its own, your underreportings or overdeductions. This is why we need to remind you of Section 6501: *Limitations on Assessment and Collection.* This is that "3-year rule" that we told you about in Chapter 3 (starting on page 3-2). Section 6501(a) means that, if you file an original return (whether on time or late), the IRS has up to three years after its receiving the return to assess you for any underpayment of tax.

Various courts have held that Section 6501 turns on the nature of one's original return, and not on an amended return. A second return, reporting an additional tax, is an amendment or supplement to the original return. It does not act to toll the limitations period which begins with the original return. Perfect accuracy or completeness on an original return is not necessary, if it evinces an honest and genuine endeavor to satisfy the law. This is true even if, at the time of filing the original return, omissions or inaccuracies are present to make the amendment necessary. [*Zellerbach Paper Co.,* 293 U.S. 172, 35-1 USTC ¶ 9003.]

A key exception to the 3-year rule is subsection 6501(e)(1)(A): *Substantial Omission of Items.* This says in part—

> *If the taxpayer omits from **gross income** an amount properly includible therein which is in excess of **25 percent** of the amount of gross income stated in the return, the tax may be assessed . . . at any time **within 6 years** after the return was filed.*

All of which means that if your unintentional omissions of income are 25 percent or less of the correct amount, the 3-year rule holds. If the omissions exceed 25 percent, a 6-year rule takes effect. This is further justification of our urging that you always file on time; you can make corrections later. Make sure, however, that your "error band" of corrections is limited to plus or minus 25 percent: income **or** deductions.

Subsection 6501(c)(7) brings out the point that, if you amend a return within 60 days of the expiration of the three-year assessment period, and there's additional tax to pay, the limitation period is extended automatically an additional 60 days. The message here is that, if you are going to amend your return — for whatever reason — you shouldn't wait until the very last three-year minute to do so.

Overview of Form 1040X

Amending a return is almost as common as filing the original return itself. Our guess is that nearly 20% of all taxpayers need to file an amended return for one reason or another. So common is this need that a special IRS form applies, namely: **Form 1040X —** *Amended U.S. Individual Income Tax Return.* As this title indicates, Form 1040X can only be used for *individual income* tax matters. There are other amending forms for entities and other types of taxes.

Form 1040X consists of two pages, front and back. It is structured to accommodate a limited number of changes to income, deductions, and credits. It can be used to correct Form 1040, Form 1040A, Form 1040EZ, Form 1040NR, etc. You must use a separate 1040X for each tax year. You cannot combine two or more tax years on one Form 1040X. Furthermore, when you sign a 1040X, you must declare that you have filed an original return for the tax year that you have designated at the top of the form.

After the name and address block on the form, you are asked the following questions:

A. *If the name or address shown above is different from that shown on the original return, check here . . .* ▶ ☐

B. *Has original return been changed or audited by the IRS or have you been notified that it will be?* ☐ Yes ☐ No *If notified that it will be, identify the IRS office* ▶ _____

The idea behind these questions is to enable the IRS to track through its system to locate your original return. It is NOT to select your return for audit. The audit selection criteria comprise a whole different process. You could have filed your original return with one service center, then moved, and filed your amended return with another service center.

The main body of Form 1040X is headed: *Income and Deductions (See Instructions)*. Basically, the instructions tell you that for every change that you enter in the preprinted lines, an explanation should appear on page 2. You are also instructed to attach all supporting documents to each change that you make. Although the instructions don't tell you so, we tell you that if you make more than three changes for a given year, your original return most likely would be audited. Even three changes, unless they are relatively minor, can expose you to the risk of audit. One or two basic changes, if adequately explained, are quite acceptable.

The changes are indicated in the center column of a 3-column format. These columns are designated:

(A)   As originally reported or as previously adjusted.
(B)   Net change: Increase or (Decrease)
(C)   Correct amount

The last few lines on page 1 of Form 1040X are subheaded: *Refund or Amount You Owe*. There are six of these lines which are clear and specific. If you show that a refund is due you, you have the option of applying all or part of that refund to your estimated tax for the next following year. If you owe money, you are expected to pay it in full when filing your amended return. The IRS will bill you for any penalty or interest due.

A general overview of page 1 of Form 1040X is presented in Figure 5.2. Our depiction is not intended to reproduce the actual form, but to convey the gist of the information required.

Many Correction Uses

Form 1040X can be used for making corrective changes to the entire Form 1040-series. There are at least eight different change-likely categories, namely:

1. Total income
2. Adjustments to income
3. Itemized deductions
4. Exemptions and filing status

Form 1040X	AMENDED INCOME TAX RETURN	Year

	Your Name & Current Address	Your Soc. Sec. No.
	Telephone Number (optional)	Spouse's Soc. Sec. No.

A — Check if address above is different from original ☐

B — Has it been changed or audited? ☐ yes ☐ no ___(identify)___

C — Check if any item is changed for a tax shelter ☐

D — Filing status claimed
Original return ▶ ☐☐☐☐
This return ▶ ☐☐☐☐

Explain Each Change on Page 2. Show Computations. Attach Supporting Schedules and Forms.

Income and Deductions		(A) As Originally Reported $	(B) CHANGE Increase (Decrease) $	(C) Correct Amount $
1	Adjusted gross income	1		
2	Deductions	2		
3	Exemptions	3		
4	Taxable income	4		
5	Tax. Method used	5		
6	Credits	6		
7	Other taxes	7		
8	Payments	8		

Total Payments ▶	
Overpayment (if any) on original return or as adjusted	▶
Subtract overpayment (if any) from total payments	▶
Compare with correct tax: AMOUNT YOU OWE	⊠
Compare with correct tax: AMOUNT OF REFUND	

Under penalties of perjury, . . . etc. . . . .

▶ _____/s/ Amender_____   date   _/s/ Spouse (if joint)_   date

Fig. 5.2 - General Format and Contents: Page 1 of Form 1040X

5. Deductible credits
6. Other taxes
7. Prepayments of tax
8. Refundable credits

By far the largest single category of change addresses the *components* of "total income." If you look at any of your recent Forms 1040, you'll note that the income block consists of some 15 different line entries of income. Most of these income lines require that a separate backup form or schedule be attached. There could be changes in any of the backup attachments which produce a refund. Business income and investment income schedules tend to be complex and confusing. These frequently lead to errors which can be corrected with Form 1040X.

For example, take the recent case of a taxpayer who had a small advertising business. He employed free-lance artists and writers. His total gross payments to these "independent contractors" for the year came to $182,650. Mistakenly, he entered $132,650 as an expense on his business schedule. It was not until the following tax year that he discovered the $50,000 error. Upon discovery, he filed Form 1040X showing a <$50,000> decrease in total income. Within 90 days, he received a refund check from the IRS for $15,360. The reason he got his refund so quickly was that he filed a *one-item* change, with self-explanatory substantiating documents attached.

When filing refund claims, it is best to stick to one, two, or three at most, straightforward self-explanatory issues. Never try to "fine tune" your original return by changing numerous small and large items on an amended return. You had your chance to do things more or less right when you filed the original return. However, if you made one or two obvious mistakes or oversights, Form 1040X is versatile and great.

Change in Filing Status

Another common change to an original return has to do with filing and dependency status. This is particularly true where spousal divorce and split-apart children are involved. In the emotion of disharmony between spouses, there is confusion as to which filing status/dependency option to pursue. The result often is that tax returns are held hostage to family conflicts. Returns either are filed late or not at all. This practice only makes matters worse, because one spouse invariably points the finger of blame at the other.

There is a general misconception that married persons (with or without children) must always file a joint return. This is NOT so. It is true that the filing of "a" return is statutorily required of every individual. But it is not true that the filing of a joint return is statutorily required. A joint return filing is elective and discretionary only. The statutory term used is *may:* not "shall."

The tax law on point is Section 6013: *Joint Returns of Income Tax by Husband and Wife.* Its subsection (a) reads in part as—

*A husband and wife **may make a single return** jointly of income taxes . . ., even though one of the spouses has neither gross income nor deductions, except . . .* [Emphasis added.]

The real clincher to this discretionary right is subsection (b): *Joint Return After Filing Separate Return.* The pertinent lead-off portion to this subsection of 6013 is—

*If an individual **has filed a separate return** for a taxable year for which a joint return could have been made by him and his spouse under subsection (a) and the time prescribed by law for filing the return for such taxable year has expired, such individual and his spouse may nevertheless make a joint return for such taxable year.* [Emphasis added.]

There is real amended-return opportunity in Section 6013(b).

Should there develop any marital disharmony between spouses who have been filing jointly over the years, either or both can file as *married separate.* The first one who does so before the April 15th date "sets the stage" — so to speak — for the other spouse who may not file or who may file late. Conceivably, this could widen the marital disharmony. Still, it is much better that one dutiful spouse file and pay on time, than to endure the emotional impasse aggravated by late filing penalties, additional taxes, and interest imposed on both spouses. Invariably, the dutiful spouse (on a joint return) winds up paying the delinquent spouse's taxes anyhow. So, he or she might as well file separately on time.

If, subsequently to one spouse's "married separate" filing, the two spouses reconcile their tax differences, the original separate return(s) can be amended to be filed jointly. This is the true virtue of Section 6013(b). The first-filing spouse has up to three years after April 15 to do so. If no spousal tax reconciliation can be made within this time frame, said spouse will have met his or her separate obligation to the IRS. It is then up to the IRS and the second-filing (or non-filing) spouse to work things out.

So important is this "married separate" filing concept that we depict it in an oversimplified way in Figure 5.3. In those unpleasant situations where marital and/or parental disharmony become an annual tug-of-war at tax filing time, a separate original return — which can be amended later — is one of the most practical taxpayer disagreeing rights that an individual has.

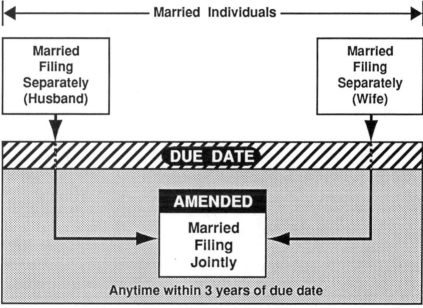

Fig. 5.3 - Amended "Cooling Off" Period for Marrieds Filing Separately

Refunds from Mismatching Notices

The IRS is quick to hassle you for any computer mismatchings that will generate more revenue for it. If the mismatchings bring to your attention overpayments and losses that you did not use, no refunds are made when you respond to the mismatching notice. We pointed out this disturbing feature to you in Chapter 4 (Step 8 on page 4-8).

The most common mismatching refund potentials derive from Forms 1099-B (Broker transactions), 1099-DIV (Dividends & distributions), 1099-INT (Interest income), and 1099-R (Retirement plans & IRAs). To help spot your refund potential, keep in mind that the CP-2000 *matching reference* is the **gross** amount reported by payer informants. As long as you match the gross amount at the proper line on your return, you are on your own thereafter. We cite a few illustrative examples.

The CP-2000 notice lists that you received Form 1099-B showing $8,625 which you did not report on your return. The 1099-B form came to you after you had already filed Form 1040. You realized a loss on the transaction (you put up $12,000), but you let it ride. "No big deal," you say to yourself. Your attitude changes, however, when the IRS hassles you for tax, penalty, and interest on the amount of $8,625 not reported.

In your response to the CP-2000 notice (and demand), you prepare and attach Schedule D (1040): *Capital Gains & Losses*. For the transaction being questioned, you show the $8,625 as *sales price* and your $12,000 as *cost or other basis*. You compute your loss at <3,375> (12,000 – 8,625). Instructions at the bottom of Schedule D limit your current year's loss to <3,000>, but allow you a <375> capital loss carryover to the following year. You clarify all of this on your CP-2000 response, then immediatly prepare and file Form 1040X. It is on Form 1040X that you compute and claim your refund on the <3,000> loss.

Probably, THE most confusing informant return is Form 1099-DIV. It contains information on gross dividends, capital gain distributions, nontaxable distributions, and ordinary dividends. Many mistakes are made using this form.

Consider, for example, the following numerical amounts on your 1099-DIV:

Gross dividends	$3,290
Capital gains	1,860
Nontaxable distributions	720
Ordinary dividends	710

You dutifully reported the $710 on Schedule B (Part II): Dividend income. You also reported the $1,860 on Schedule D. You did not report the $720 because it is not taxable.

Some 18 months later, you get a CP-2000 notice that you failed to report $3,290 on Schedule B (Part II). Additional tax, penalty, and interest are assessed. The notice did not acknowledge your reporting the $710 nor the $1,860, nor that you did not have to report the $720. You correct the IRS computer by reporting the $3,290 on Schedule B (Part II). You immediately subtract from it the $1,860 plus $720 (total: 2,580). The taxable result is the same $710 (3,290 – 2,580) that you reported in the first place. No additional tax is due.

The effort that you went through to correct the IRS irritates you. As a consequence, you decide to examine more closely your Schedule B (Part I): Interest income. You find that you overreported $850 as interest income from a friend to whom you had loaned $6,000. The $850, it turns out, was partial repayment of principal: not interest. Repayment on principal is tax treated as "return of capital": not taxed. You now have a basis for claiming a refund via Form 1040X.

The above example illustrates an everyday computer matching fact that you probably didn't know about. When you overreport an income amount, inadvertently or otherwise, **even when obvious** to the IRS through its CP-2000 matching program, you are NOT informed of said fact. This IRS "one-wayness" injects a new response mentality towards CP-2000 notices. **Any time** you receive a CP-2000 notice from the IRS, you should regard it as a challenge to look for errors and oversights on the IRS's part.

Loss Carryback Refunds

Special sections of the tax code permit certain types of losses to be carried back to one or more years *preceding* the actual loss event. For example, two such sections are:

Sec. 165(i) — Disaster Losses: Election to Take Deduction in Preceding Year

Sec. 172(b) — Net Operating Loss Carrybacks and Carryovers

These carryback options require the filing of Form 1040X for each eligible carryback year. Although the loss is sustained in a current year, it is the carryback year return which is amended: not the loss year return.

Section 165(i) addresses those substantial losses to property (personal or business) caused by natural disasters (fire, flood, storm, tornado, hurricane, earthquake, etc.). These events warrant a Presidential Declaration under the Disaster Relief and Emergency Assistance Act. For each property loss, the amount recognized for tax purposes is computed on Form 4684: *Casualties and Thefts*. The amount of loss is attached to Form 1040X for the taxable year *immediately preceding* the taxable year in which the disaster occurred.

Section 172(b) addresses those ordinary operating losses caused by unforeseen events in a competitive business environment. Not every trade or business operates year after year at a profit. Invariably, there are some "bad" years. For some inexplicable reason, products, services, and merchandise cannot be sold or cannot be sold in sufficient quantities to turn a profit. For these situations, net operating losses (NOLs) result. To compute the amount of loss, Schedule A (Form 1045): *Net Operating Loss for Carrybacks*, is required. For each NOL year, subsection 172(b)(1)(A)(i) enables the loss to be carried back . . . *to each of the 3 taxable years preceding* the taxable year of such loss. For losses occurring **after August 5, 1997** the carryback period is reduced to two years (instead of three). However, the 2-year carryback applies not only to NOLs but to losses resulting from fire, storm, or other casualty.The mechanism for claiming these losses is the filing of Form 1040X *separately* for each carryback year.

All loss carrybacks result in a decrease in tax for the carryback year. This means that a much needed refund is due the loss-sustained taxpayer. Although the amount of refund (with interest) never compensates dollar-for-dollar for the actual loss, it does help soften the financial blow in time of need.

6

EXAMINATION NOTICES

IRS's Power To Select Your Tax Return For Audit Is Embodied In Code Section 7602: EXAMINATION OF BOOKS AND WITNESSES. An "Office Audit" Lasts About 2 To 3 Hours, Whereas A "Field Audit" Lasts 2 To 3 DAYS. The Selection Process Is Based On Secret Formulas Of Computer Discriminate Functions, Known As "DIF-Scoring." The Formulas Use Taxpayer PROFILES Which Often Cause Repetitive Audits Of The Same Individual. You Cannot Protest Against An Audit. However, You Do Have Appointment And Representation Rights. Together With The Target Year Of Audit, Your Prior- And Subsequent-Year Returns May ALSO Be Examined.

An "examination notice" is a computer-printed letter informing you that your tax return for a designated year has been computer selected for audit. The computer selection is based on the *probability* that a human examination of your return will produce substantial additional revenue for the coffers of government. The examination is performed by IRS employees classed as "tax auditors" or "revenue agents," depending on the type of examination.

The IRS prefers using the term *examination* of a return rather than *audit* of a return. The two terms have the same additional revenue objectives. But the implications differ slightly. An examination is softer in tone than an audit. An examination implies inspection, testing, and interrogation in a way that if you get a passing grade, you are free and clear. An audit, on the other hand, implies some wrongdoing. Because of possible wrongdoing, it becomes necessary to scrutinize your accounts, records, and claims with the express intention of making adjustments.

Either way, whether it's an examination or audit of your return, the IRS's objective is to stick you for more money. It is **not** to give you a pat on the back for being a good citizen, or to reward you for paying high taxes. The nearest you'll ever get to a pat on the back is a computer printout: *Thank you for your cooperation.*

All tax audits are time consuming and irritating. It takes time to prepare for the audit, it takes time to answer the personal and financial questions, it takes time to organize and present the documentation needed, and it takes time for an auditor to examine thoroughly chosen items on your return. The more time an auditor spends on your return, the more money he/she may find.

Audits are irritating because most auditors are not very communicative. They tend to be picky-picky; their comprehension of the real world is rather limited. They are basically "bean counters." They see only black beans or white beans. When they encounter grey beans, they interpret them as black or white, whichever produces the higher tax.

With the above in mind, our focus in this chapter is on the procedural aspects of an audit; it is not on the nitty-gritty of tax law interpretation. Whatever the additional tax outcome will be, will be. There are ways to appeal adverse outcomes, which we'll get into in the next chapter. Our thesis in this chapter is that, by reducing your time and irritation of an audit, you'll be in a stronger position to appeal, should that be necessary. It is your disagreement rights — and their limitations — during an audit that we focus on here.

The Selection Process

When a tax return is received at any of 10 IRS processing centers, it is "eyeballed" for completeness. That is, human scanners glance through it, simply to see that all required attachments and schedules are there. They quick-check the applicable entry lines and the checked checkboxes. They look to see that the return is properly signed. If acceptable, they date stamp it and assign it a Document Locator Number. All of this is purely an acceptance procedure which has nothing to do with audit selection.

Audit selection is based primarily on a highly sophisticated computer program called: DIF Scoring (DIF = Discriminant

Information Function). Based on many years of audit experience, the IRS classifies all individual taxpayers into categorical "profiles." Within each profile class, there are certain items on a return which tend to be overstated in the taxpayer's favor and understated in the IRS's favor. These test items become the *discriminate functions* which the computer uses to arrive at a mathematical DIF score. High DIF scores have high probability for audit; low DIF scores do not. The general scheme is presented in Figure 6.1.

Approximately 90% of all audit selections are made on the basis of DIF scores. The other 10% or so are based on (a) prime issue analysis, (b) special informant reports, and (c) vendettas against high-profile taxpayers. The final selection is made at each IRS District Office depending on its case load. There are some 35 such offices throughout the United States.

Prime-issue analysis is also a computer selection program, after a DIF score has been assigned. A "prime issue" is an item which affects a multitude of taxpayers (regardless of their profiles) because the tax law on point is vague or ambiguous. The Prime Issue Analysis program "red flags" those returns where the IRS has interpreted the ambiguity for maximum revenue. For low-DIF returns, the prime issue selection generally results in a *correspondence* audit. That is, the taxpayer is sent a letter, called a "correction notice," with limited opportunity to respond and rebut. At this stage, most taxpayers give in and pay. No real audit actually ensues.

Under the special informant program, a taxpayer whistleblows on another taxpayer who is alleged to be violating the tax laws. The IRS encourages whistleblowing through Section 7623 of the IR Code and its Form 211: *Application for Reward for Original Information*. The informed-on taxpayer is almost certain to be audited. But before the IRS does so, it usually audits the informant first. This way, it gets *two* maximum revenues with very little selection effort on its part.

Under the personal vendetta program, high-profile taxpayers who have gotten under the skin of irate IRS officials and agents can be especially selected for audit. Vendetta selectees are usually professional-level taxpayers who have the intellect and stamina to stand up to IRS bullying and challenge its interpretation of a tax law. Also included are "tax protesters" who publicly chastise the IRS for what they perceive to be its unconstitutional behavior. For these selectees, their DIF scores are irrelevant. The IRS contrives audit cases to teach its vendetta selectees "a lesson."

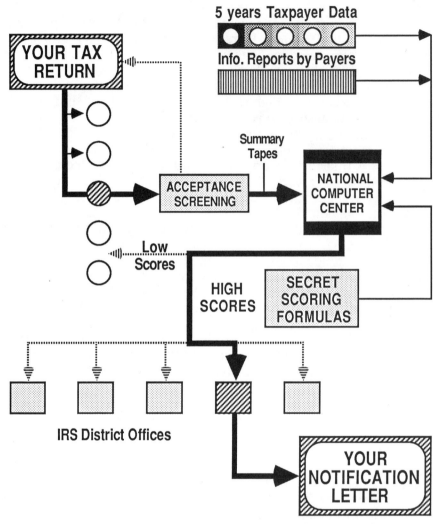

Fig.6.1 - Schematic Overview of Audit Selection Process

Two Types of Audits

As the IRS becomes more computer sophisticated, we can all expect more computer "communications" from it. However, not every computer printout is notification of an audit. Much of it is routine screening for acceptability of returns, corrections of arithmetic, and matching of income information. These are not — repeat, *not* — audit selection proceedings. Many taxpayers are so terrified of the IRS that they construe every computer form sent to them as being an audit.

Regardless of the type of computer form sent to you, an examination notice is quite specific in its opening sentence. In one variant or another, the selection notice will state—

Your Federal tax return has been. . . selected for **examination**.

So, unless the IRS computer printout uses the word "examine" or "examination" (somewhere) in its very first sentence, you are not under audit. Any other communication you may have received is no pre-indication of an audit.

The power of the IRS to examine *any tax return* is set forth in **Section 7602**: *Examination of Books and Witnesses*. Once selected for audit, you cannot refuse to go through with the process. You may disagree with the initially proposed time and place, but that's all.

Basically, there are two kinds of audit examination. There is the *office* audit, and the *field* audit. The difference is in the location and duration of audit.

An office audit takes place at the nearest IRS office in the general vicinity of the taxpayer's residence. This means that the taxpayer — and/or his representative (if any) — must gather up the pertinent books and records and trudge in to an IRS office. Often, two visits are required. The first visit lasts about one and one-half hours. The second visit is a follow-up to the first, where all of the needed substantiation was not available then, or where the auditor requests new information for which you were not prepared. As we said earlier, much of this is time consuming and aggravating.

A field audit takes place at the taxpayer's place of business, or where he keeps his primary business records and files. Field audits focus on those taxpayers who are in a trade or business, such as in a proprietorship, partnership, or corporate form. These audits typically take a day and a half to two days for the auditor's first visit. The second and "conferencing" visit takes about a half-day.

Office Audit Notice

With all of its computer hardware and software at its fingertips, the IRS still dumbs things up. It still hasn't learned that taxpayers need some headliner bold type to give them a clue as to what the "correspondence" is all about.

When a taxpayer opens the brown, window-type envelope, he finds the computer message to be all in small print. There's no salutation nor subject reference: just the taxpayer's name and address, and a lot of white space. The white space causes the eyes to glaze as they read, fumble, and try to figure out what the small print is all about. This experience alone is upsetting and irritating.

Therefore, when you receive a small-print computer letter from the IRS, the first thing to do is: Take a deep breath. Then slowly, calmly, and deliberately read the opening sentence. Stop there. Then go back and reread it.

If the first sentence starts out with *"We selected,"* and mentions the word *"examine,"* you have an office audit on your hands. The full sentence reads—

> *We selected your Federal Income Tax return for the year shown below to examine the items listed at the end of this letter.*

This particular sentence puts you on official notice that certain items on your return **will be** examined. You have no choice in these items. You have other choices, but not as to what will or will not be examined. At this point, you have no right of protest or appeal.

The rest of the opening paragraph gives you a modest option, namely: your appointment date and time. The second, third, and fourth sentences read—

> *Please call us at the number shown above to arrange a convenient appointment. It is important that you contact our office **within 10 days** from the date of this letter. For your convenience, we have provided space below to record your appointment:*
>
> *Date_____ Time_____ Place_____*

You are expected to phone within 10 days. If you do not, don't be surprised if you get a subsequent computer letter disallowing all the audit items listed and demanding payment due. You are not expected to undergo audit within 10 days; just to phone to set up your appointment.

The name and phone number given at the top of the notice (right-hand corner) is that of the Appointment Clerk. It is *not* the auditor.

In an office audit, there is no preassignment of tax examiners. Whoever happens to be around on the date and hour of your appointment takes your case. If you have any audit questions at the time you set your appointment, the clerk will take your message and some examiner will get back in touch with you.

Other features of an office examination notice are presented in Figure 6.2. The IRS tries to make these notices informal in tone, so as not to upset taxpayers too much.

Field Audit Notice

In field audits, a revenue agent is preassigned to your case. That agent's name (and phone number) appears at the top of the notice letter and also at the bottom. Sometimes the notice letter is signed or initialed by the IRS agent, but most times not.

The small-print computer instructions to you are brief and pointed. A proposed date and time for the audit is picked by the agent, and you are simply asked to confirm it or arrange another. The place of appointment is at your place of business as designated on the business portion of your tax return. It is not at your personal residence, unless such residence also happens to be your place of business.

The first sentence of a field audit notice reads succinctly as—

Your Federal Income Tax Return has been assigned to me for examination.

That's it! It's a fait accompli. You have no say in the matter. The tax year and tax form (and schedules) are conspicuously indicated.

The rest of the opening paragraph reads—

I would like to meet with you on the following date, time, and place. Please call within 10 days to confirm the appointment, or to arrange another appointment.

What happens if you object to meeting with the preassigned revenue agent? He or she simply disallows all of the audit items that have been pre-selected for examination.

When the agent stereotypes that "I would like to meet with you," he also expects you to provide him a temporary place to work at your place of business. You are not required to give up your own desk for this, nor are you expected to displace any of your

Department of Treasury
Internal Revenue Service
DISTRICT DIRECTOR
Address: _____
District No.: _____

YOUR SSN: _____
Date of Notice: _____
IRS Phone No.: _____
Appt. Clerk: _____

YOUR NAME AND ADDRESS

[1] We have selected your Federal Income Tax Return for the year shown below ... **for examination.** -
APPOINTMENT INFORMATION

Tax Year _____ **Place** _____ **Room No.** _____

[2] To avoid unnecessary repetitive examinations - - - - - - - - - - - - - - - - - -

[3] You may have someone represent you [with Form 2848] - - - - - - - - - -

[4] We have included **information paragraphs** to assist you - - - - -

[5] If we propose any changes, we will explain them - - - - - - - - - - - - - - -

[6] When you come for your appointment, please bring this letter - - - - -
Thank you for your cooperation.

Sincerely yours,

/s/ [facsimile]_____

IRS District Director

ENCLOSURES
- Information Paragraphs : I, II, III
- Notice 609 : Privacy and Paperwork Reduction Acts
- Publication I : Your Rights as a Taxpayer

Fig.6.2 - Format and Contents of Office Examination Notice

employees or associates. Pick some working space that's out of the way, and out of sight of your employees or associates, and clear away enough room for the auditor to do his or her thing uninterrupted.

All field agents are instructed to request a tour of your business facilities, so as to observe first-hand your operations. Don't read anything sinister into this unless the auditor gets too nosey and too demanding. Unless the auditor has been tipped-off about some illegal activity of yours, he simply wants to eyeball your premises, see what kind of furnishings and equipment you have, and note any lavish decor that might imply extensive personal and family use of your business premises.

Interview Procedures

Some persons get upset at the whole examination process, and allege that it is nothing but harassment. They may also allege that it is "unconstitutional" because a person is presumed innocent until proven guilty.

That may be, but the examination of a tax return is **not** an innocent versus guilty issue. It is an issue of whether or not certain items — those selected by the IRS — are correct on your return. Within bounds, the IRS is empowered to examine whatever items on your return it has chosen to examine. The term "within bounds," however, is quite vague. Often, revenue agents, more so than tax auditors, cross the bounds into unconstitutional territory. Government agents with tax power are not always prudent and mindful of their constitutional limits.

To help protect taxpayers against examination abuses, Section 7521 was enacted in 1988. This section, titled: *Procedures Involving Taxpayer Interviews*, addresses such matters as—

1. Recording of interviews — audio only, not video, may be made by taxpayer or IRS.
2. Explanation of process — with preprinted handouts.
3. Right of consultation — at any time during interview.
4. Right of representation — without actually appearing at interview.

When first proposed, Section 7521 was intended to address "Reasonable time and place" for examination interviews. The Congressional proposal included such statements as—

It is generally not reasonable for the IRS to require a taxpayer to attend an examination at an IRS office other than the one located closest to the taxpayer's home. Similarly, it is generally not reasonable for the IRS to audit a taxpayer at his or her place of business if the business is so small that doing so essentially requires the taxpayer to close the business. The committee anticipates that in determining the reasonableness of time and place of an interview, regulations will take into account the possibility of physical danger to an IRS agent.

Because of the widespread public antagonism that the IRS has generated for itself, its employees are always aware of the possibility of physical danger to themselves. As a consequence, rather elaborate security screening procedures are instituted before an examination takes place. All time and place matters are resolved ahead of time by mail and phone. When an auditee appears at an IRS office, he must first identify himself, his purpose and time, through a system of intercom phone and buzzer signals. If an audit is to be conducted at the taxpayer's place of business, the auditor makes a preliminary surveillance dry run past the taxpayer's premises to assure himself/herself of the safety prospects.

So concerned is the IRS about danger to its officials and employees that it prevailed upon Congress to add subsection (d) to Section 7521. This one-sentence provision reads—

This section [7521] shall not apply to criminal investigations or investigations relating to the integrity of any officer or employee of the Internal Revenue Service.

In other words, the Section 7521 procedures apply only to those "routine examinations" of cooperative taxpayers. In these situations, issues of place, time, and safety are mutually recognized as ordinary civil courtesies.

Explanation of Processes

The principal virtue of Section 7521 lies in its subsection (b): *Safeguards* [for Taxpayers]. This subsection consists of two paragraphs, namely:

(1) *Explanations of Processes*, and
(2) *Right of Consultation.*

There are also subsections (a): Right of Recording, and (c): Right of Representation. The audio recording of an IRS examination or collection interview is not very productive. It adds an element of guarded formality and materially slows down the process. If a particularly offensive accusation or threat has been made by the IRS interviewer, the taxpayer can always make a handwritten notation to himself/herself for amplification later, should the need arise. As to your "right of representation," we'll comment later.

All IRS interviewers now have to follow the procedures prescribed in subsection 7521(b)(1)(A) and (B). The statutory requirement states (in pertinent part) that—

An officer or employee of the [IRS] *shall before or at an initial interview provide to the taxpayer—*

(A) an explanation of the audit process and the taxpayer's rights [thereunder]*, or*
(B) an explanation of the collection process and the taxpayer's rights [thereunder].

In practice, these "explanations" are perfunctory and hurried. They are accompanied by such preprinted handouts as:

Pub. 1   — *Your Rights as a Taxpayer*, or
Pub. 594   — *Understanding the Collection Process.*

Experience has shown that the IRS does not follow the spirit of its "Rights Publications," though such publications do indeed meet the letter of the law.

As to Paragraph (2) above: Right of Consultation, the IRS is less than straightforward. The interviewer rarely mentions — let alone explains — what is meant by your right of consultation. So that you'll be forewarned, the precise statutory wording of Code Sec. 7521(b)(2) is—

*If the taxpayer **clearly states** to an officer or employee of the* [IRS] *at any time during an interview . . . that* [he] *wishes to consult with . . . any person permitted to represent* [him] *before the* [IRS]*, such officer or employee **shall suspend** such interview regardless of whether the taxpayer may have answered one or more questions.* [Emphasis added.]

The implication here is that once you realize you may be in over your head, you can request that the interview be suspended — but only temporarily — until you can get professional counseling on the issue(s) raised. Obviously, you cannot use your right of consultation to create unreasonable delay or hindrance to the IRS. If you do, the IRS can ignore your right and assess the maximum possible tax and penalties. This is called: *The No Response Procedure.*

The Betting Strategy

Every IRS auditor has the power to raise any issue on a return that he or she deems suspect. Generally, however, office auditors stick to the list of items indicated in the official examination notice. The last phrase in the opening sentence of such notice reads: *to examine the items listed at the end of this letter.* Then another portion of the letter reads:

We have included information paragraphs to assist you in selecting the type of documents required to substantiate the items. It will save time if you keep together the records related to each item.

Strategically, the computer designates at least three categories of items. One is the "target item," and the other two are alternate "cover-our-bet" items. The target item is usually the one that trips the selection of your return. It is the one category that the IRS is 85% confident it will scoop up substantial additional revenue.

The two alternate items are for fallback purposes. They cover that 15% chance that the genie computer has mis-scored you. It's a hedging policy: "As long as we have your attention, we might as well check these other two items." It's a form of **betting strategy** that the IRS uses on all audits: office and field. The concept is illustrated in Figure 6.3.

This Figure 6.3 strategy applies principally to the audit (target) year. This is the year specifically indicated on the face of the examination notice. At the very end of the list of the items for examination, an instruction reads—

Please bring to the interview a copy of your ___(prior)___ and ___(subsequent)___ returns.

Thus, if your audit year is 1998, for example, you'll be asked to bring also your 1997 and 1999 returns. The examination notice will

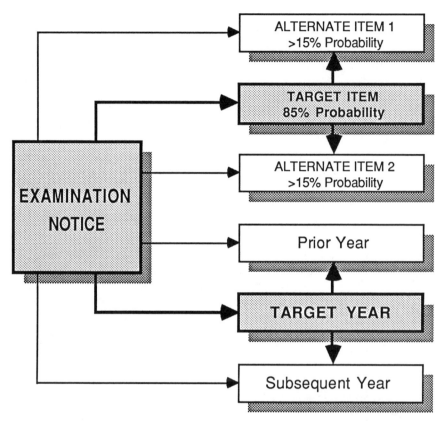

Fig. 6.3 - IRS's Betting Strategy on All Audits

be sent to you after mid-2000, such that your 1999 return will have been filed by then.

If the targeted item for the target year results in a substantial change (additional tax), the auditor will automatically scan your prior-year and subsequent-year returns for the same listed item. This is the IRS's way of bagging several birds with one stone.

Repetitive Audits?

Because "profiling" is the reference norm for DIF scoring programs, taxpayers in certain occupations or businesses are DIF-selected repetitively, year after year. It is not uncommon for an outside salesman, for example, to receive audit notifications every other year or so, ten years in a row. This is blatant IRS harassment.

One would think that after all of these years, the DIF programming could be modified to take into account prior audits and prior results.

The nearest statutory protection that a taxpayer has against repetitive audits is Section 7605(b): ***Restrictions on Examination***. This section reads—

> *No taxpayer shall be subjected to unnecessary examination or investigations, and only one inspection of a taxpayer's books of account shall be made for each taxable year . . . unless the [IRS], after investigation notifies the taxpayer in writing that an additional inspection is necessary.*

Like so many other things in the tax code and official policy, the fine-point interpretations are left entirely up to the IRS. It can examine the same person year after year after year, if it wants to. Many of the repetitive audits are "necessary" make-work projects for the training of IRS personnel, particularly its field agents.

In an *office* audit notification, the second paragraph reads—

> *To avoid an unnecessary repetitive examination, let the appointment clerk know as soon as possible if your income tax return was examined for the same items listed at the end of this letter and the examination resulted in no change to your tax liability in either of the two prior years.*

The way to let the appointment clerk know about your repetitive audits is to first phone, and then follow up with a factually worded letter. List all prior years audited, the items at issue each year, the additional tax dollars each year (if any), and the number of hours the IRS spent on the audit each year. Attach the pertinent IRS documents: the prior-year(s) audit notification(s) and the results of the prior audit(s). Show the totals and recite your concluding facts.

Here's a true case example. The taxpayer, an outside salesman, had been audited five times in a 9-year period. The IRS spent 16 hours on the audits and recovered a total of $320 in additional tax. That's a return of just $20 for each IRS audit hour. This is not a very efficient examination/collection process. The IRS's performance target (quotas?) for its office examiners is $200 or more in additional revenue per audit hour.

In this particular repetitive case, the IRS responded as follows:

After consideration of all available facts [that you have presented], *we have determined that:*

☒   *We will **not** continue with the examination of your return.*

The IRS will never discontinue a *field* audit, no matter how clear-cut your repetitive audit case is. There are two reasons for this. One, the performance target is $2,000 per day (i.e., $250 per hour). Secondly, because of the multitude and complexities of issues on a business return, even the most incompetent auditor can find something to force an increase in tax.

Field Agent Elitism

Depending on the targeted examination issues, there are three different pay grades of IRS agents assigned to field audits. The three grades are: (a) revenue agents, (b) special agents, and (c) enforcement agents. A revenue agent is empowered to examine any and all business entries on a return, and to inspect the business premises for conformity to the return. A special agent is empowered to go beyond the return, and probe personal and financial matters based on his suspicion of fraud or tax evasion activities. He may enter the business premises unannounced, day or night, whenever the business is open. An enforcement agent is empowered to carry firearms, execute search warrants, make arrests without warrants, and seize any property (day or night) of a taxpayer who has committed, or is committing, a tax felony.

All three grades of these agents constitute the *elite corps* of the IRS. As with all elitists, they tend to be arrogant, pushy, and overbearing. Their trained cynicisms and personal whims often get the best of them. This is especially true of special agents and enforcement agents.

The most common form of field examination of a return is conducted by a revenue agent. Even this person's power is quite awesome.

If you take an office examination letter (Figure 6.2) and place it alongside a field examination letter, you can notice an immediate difference in tone. The field letter is short and brisk. Between its computer-printed official lines, there is a sense of compulsion about it. There is less solicitation of your cooperation and more the tone of command. It is a *summons* which, indirectly, says: "I am your god; you must obey." The name of the revenue agent in command is clearly displayed.

Attached to the summons is Form 4564: *Information Document Request*. It lists, at minimum, 10 categories of items for which you are expected to have all documents ready for a 2-day examination visit. We present in Figure 6.4 a recent real-life example of this document request. For Figure 6.4 purposes, a "document" is a self-explanatory statement or invoice consisting of one or more pages as necessary. One year of bank statements, for example, consists of 12 documents. All total, the Figure 6.4 auditee (taxpayer) produced 192 separate documents! How would **you** fare with a Figure 6.4-type request?

Role of Representative

Both types of examination notices inform you that you may have a tax professional represent you. The office notice states (slightly edited) that—

You may keep the appointment yourself or have someone else represent you. If you are not present, you must furnish your representative a written authorization, namely, Form 2848: Power of Attorney and Declaration of Representative.

The field notice is more brusque; it says—

If you prefer to be represented, please provide us with a properly executed Form 2848: Power of Attorney and Declaration of Representative.

Both examination notices are the consequence of Section 7521(c): *Representatives Holding Power of Attorney.* Such persons may be—

Any attorney, certified public accountant, enrolled agent, enrolled actuary, or any other person permitted to represent the taxpayer before the [IRS].

You may appoint more than one representative at the same time. The power-of-attorney form requires that you sign an "Acts Authorized" statement that—

```
┌─────────────────────────────────────────────────────────────┐
│ Form   INFORMATION DOCUMENT REQUEST    │ Date of Request      │
│ 4564                                   │ _____             │
├────────────────────────────────────────┬──────────────────────┤
│ TO:  Name of Taxpayer:_____  │ Subject:_____   │
│      Name of Business:_____  │ SSN or TIN:_____  │
└────────────────────────────────────────┴──────────────────────┘
```

Description of Documents Requested

1. All income Forms W-2, 1099, and K-1.
2. Bank statements, cancelled checks, and deposit slips for all bank accounts: business AND personal.
3. All savings accounts (passbooks, CD's, T-Bills, etc.).
4. All investment accounts (mutual funds, brokerage firms, private parties).
5. Records of any nontaxable income received (loans, gifts, inheritances, insurance, sales, etc.).
6. All workpapers used to prepare and reconcile your return.
7. Verification of Schedule C Gross Receipts.
8. Verification of Schedule C Cost of Goods Sold.
9. Invoices on all depreciable assets acquired during year.
10. Verification of the following Schedule C expenses:

    a. Advertising
    b. Car & truck
    c. Freight & postage
    d. Legal & professional
    e. Insurance   For Tax Year
    f. Rent   **1996**
    g. Repairs
    h. Supplies
    i. Office expense
    j. Travel

ALSO, PRIOR AND SUBSEQUENT TAX RETURNS (_1995_ **and** _1997_ **).**

```
┌──────────────────────────────────────────┬─────────────────────┐
│ FROM:  Name and Title of Requester        │ Information Due By:  │
│              _____, REVENUE AGENT   │ ☐ Appointment        │
│        IRS office and Phone No.            │ ☐ Mail In            │
│        _____                │                      │
└──────────────────────────────────────────┴─────────────────────┘
```

Fig. 6.4 - Example of Requested Documents for Field Audit

The representatives are authorized to receive and inspect confidential tax information and to perform any and all acts that I (we) can perform with respect to the tax matters described above, [such as] *the authority to sign any agreement, consents, or other documents* [except] *the power to receive refund checks or the power to sign certain returns.*

In the "Tax Matters" portion of the form, you must indicate the type of tax, tax form number (including attached schedules), and the year(s) or period(s) involved. You may also indicate other specific additions or deletions to the general power you have assigned.

Even though you may appoint a tax professional to represent you, it is not a bad idea for you to accompany the representative yourself. That is, you accompany him or her as an *observer*: not as the primary participant. This way, not only do you gain valuable experience in the audit process, you can also evaluate the extent of knowledge and expertise of the representative in your behalf. A seasoned representative will instruct you NOT TO ANSWER THE AUDITOR, until the representative indicates that it is all right to do so. Oftentimes, you may answer without realizing what the auditor is really getting at. A representative can often rephrase a question for you, so that you don't box yourself into a tax corner. Auditors are unforgiving when you fall into their tax traps.

A representative cannot work magic for you. He (or she) has very limited negotiation leverage. He cannot negotiate away any blatant omission of income. Nor can he justify a deduction or expense which is frivolous, without merit, or without adequate documentation. About the best he can do is: (a) properly organize the tax information requested, (b) anticipate any trick questions the auditor might ask, and (c) explain any questionable items within the context of an alternative interpretation of tax law.

A representative, for example, cannot protest the examination process just because it may be upsetting and irritating to you. Big Brother has the power to penalize your representative as well as to penalize you.

7

APPEALING AUDIT RESULTS

If You Do Not Agree With An Examiner's Report Of Income Tax Changes, You Can Opt To Appeal Within The IRS. There Is No Official Form For This. Your Written Protest Must Contain These Specifics: (a) Request For **APPEALS CONFERENCE,** (b) Identity Of Unagreed Matters, (c) Listing Of Pertinent Facts, And (d) Citation Of Applicable Law. If Acknowledged By IRS Appeals Office Within 6 Months Of The 3-Year Statute Of Limitations, You Will Be Pressed To Sign Waiver Form 872 For 12 Months' Extension. Do Not Expect Much From The Appeals Process For Disputed Amounts Exceeding $10,000.

More than 70% of all audit examinations result in a tax increase (additional tax) to the taxpayer. The IRS is trying to increase this percentage by training its auditors to recharacterize certain items — such as capitalizing the dollar amount of a substantiated item instead of allowing it to be expensed — so as to intentionally force an audit change. Then the IRS uses its audit change statistics to pressure Congress for more staff, and more tax laws. Tax professionals recognize recharacterization for what it really is. It is a *safe harbor* position for auditors when they cannot find anything else of substance to change.

By and large, though, most audit changes (increase in taxes) come about through one or more of the following situations:

1. Omission of income

2. Inadequate substantiation
3. Disallowance by interpretation
4. Disallowance when in doubt
5. Whipsaw issues

We'll define and exemplify these audit-change situations later.

All audit changes are communicated to the auditee in a written report: *Income Tax Examination Changes*. If you agree with all of the changes, you might as well skip this chapter. But if you disagree with any of the changes, this chapter can be helpful to you. That is, provided your disagreement constitutes a good faith concern about the correctness of the audit results.

In this chapter, we want to tell you about the appeals process *within* the IRS. We will tell how to proceed, what approach to take, and what to expect. Right off, we should tell you not to expect miracles. IRS Appeals Officers have only limited authority to re-examine an issue. Rarely do they reverse an auditor completely, though they may "give a little" here or there, in order to settle the matter without litigation.

Audit Change Transmittal

In most cases (field audits may be an exception), a report of income tax examination changes is mailed to each auditee (including his/her spouse) with an official transmittal letter. This transmittal is called a "30-day" letter. It is called this because if you do not respond within 30 days, the audit changes are assessed and immediate collection begins. "Immediate collection" means: demands, levies, and liens. It is for this reason that the date of the letter is separately displayed in its upper left-hand corner.

The audit change transmittal letter is approximately 350 words in length, and arranged in several paragraphs. Like most official notices from the IRS, it has no heading: no quick-identifying title. You have to begin reading to find out what it is all about. As a quick overview of its format and contents, we present Figure 7.1. Paragraph 1 reads in full as follows:

We are enclosing two copies of our report, Income Tax Examination Changes, explaining the changes we made to your return. Please read this report and decide whether you agree or disagree.

District Director, IRS

| Date: _____ |

Tax Year(s): _____
Person to Contact: _____
Phone Contact: _____
Contact Address: _____
_____

Your Name
& Address

[1] Enclosed are two copies of . . . [examination report] _ _ _ _ _ _ _ _ _ _ _

[2] If you agree, sign, date, etc. _

[3] If you agree but can't pay, contact _

[4] If you don't agree, you have 30 days _ _ _ _ _ _ _ _ _ _ _ _ _ _ _ _ _ _ _

[5] The enclosed Publication 5 explains your appeal rights.

[6] If we do not hear from you within 30 days _ _ _ _ _ _ _ _ _ _ _ _ _ _ _ _ _

[7] If you have any questions, please phone _ _ _ _ _ _ _ _ _ _ _ _ _ _ _ _ _ _

Sincerely,

Enclosures
•
•
•

/s/ _____
District Director

Fig. 7.1 - Contents of Audit Change Transmittal Letter

The enclosed report is a five- to ten-page computer printout showing recomputations of your tax and — of course, as always — the assertion of some penalty (mostly negligence). A summary of the recomputations is given on the first page of the report

Look for the line saying: **Balance Due,** and for the line saying: **Penalties.** If the total of these two lines is less than a few hundred dollars, disagreeing is probably not worth the effort. You might as well sign off and consent to the additional assessment.

If the balance due and penalties exceed $1,000, you may want to disagree and protest. The instructions for doing this are not very clear. You can, if you want, phone the auditor and discuss matters with him or her. You won't get much satisfaction, particularly in the case of a field audit. So you had better read up on your rights of appeal in the enclosures to the Figure 7.1-type letter.

Basically, you have 30 days from the audit report to appeal within the IRS. If you intend to appeal, do make telephone contact within about 10 days to let the auditor know that you do not accept his or her findings. Don't engage in any discussion about your reasons. However, do request that your phone contact date be recorded. The IRS has a bad habit of dating its notices on one date, and sending them out days and weeks later.

Paragraph 5 in Figure 7.1 directs your attention to IRS Publication 5. This publication is titled: *Appeal Rights and Preparation of Protests for Unagreed Cases*. Obviously, you want to read the part which starts with: *If You Don't Agree*. We expand on this part below.

Appeal Within 30 Days

Paragraph 4 of Figure 7.1 says (in part)—

If you do not accept our findings and do not want to take either of the above actions, you may write or call us within 30 days from the date of this letter to request a conference with an Appeals Officer. The Appeals Officer will be someone who has not examined your return and will contact you regarding the time and place for the conference. [Emphasis added.]

Farther down in the transmittal letter, it says in crucial part:

If you don't take any of the above actions within 30 days, we will process your case based on the enclosed report. You will then receive a statutory notice of deficiency that allows you 90 days to petition the U.S. Tax Court.

Thus, if you take no action within 30 days of the audit change transmittal letter, you may lose your right to appeal within the IRS. The IRS has three years to examine your return, but you have only 30 days to appeal the results of the examination.

If you intend to appeal, do so. Don't dither around. You should have started thinking about appeal when the auditor first discussed any of his/her findings with you. You should have then sized up the auditor as being picky-picky, unreasonable, or one who likes to throw his/her weight around.

The *If You Don't Agree* paragraph of Publication 5 says (in part)—

> *If you decide not to agree with the examiner's findings, . . . we urge you to appeal your case within the Service.* [However], *appeals conferences are not available to taxpayers whose reasons for disagreement do not come* **within the scope of the internal revenue laws.** *For example, disagreement based solely on moral, religious, political, constitutional, conscientious, or similar grounds* [are not appealable within the IRS]. [Emphasis added.]

Example Appealable Issues

You may want to appeal within the IRS strictly for the instructional challenge of it. Such appeals are handled by a regional Appeals Office which is independent from your local District Director or Service Center Director. Appeals conferences are conducted in an informal manner.

In most examinations, IRS auditors are not as fully versed in tax law and regulations as they should be. Nor do they give a hoot about national policy pronouncements on reasonableness and fairness. As far as the frontliners are concerned, they have a job to do. And, that's that. Every item on a return is either all black or all white; there is no grey. When you sense that there is no give by the auditor, you should prepare yourself to appeal.

At the beginning of this chapter, we listed the kinds of issues that could be appealable. We want to describe each one just briefly, so that you can get some orientation for your own approach:

Omission of Income. Not all income is taxable. The Internal Revenue Code lists approximately 50 types of income (Sections 101-150) which are not taxable. Examples are certain death benefits, gifts and inheritances, interest on state and local bonds, compensation for injuries or sickness, return of capital, and so on. Overzealous — and unknowledgeable — auditors force you to disclose all types of income: taxable and nontaxable alike. You, yourself, may not know which is nontaxable. After the audit report, you had better research this on your own.

Inadequate Substantiation. Many auditors are lazy and not too up to date in the real world. There are some situations in tax and fiscal life that they just don't comprehend. You could have a perfectly deductible item of (say) $2,345 but you can only come up with $865 in black/white documentation. The auditor will automatically disallow $1,480 (2,345 – 865). At appeal you can reconstruct the missing information by indirect means.

Disallowance by Interpretation. When an auditor perceives that you have derived some personal benefit in a business expense environment, he will disallow the whole item as a personal expense. Whether it is personal or business is simply his interpretation of the circumstances. At appeal, you have a chance to come up with more convincing evidence of the business purpose of the expenditure.

Disallowance When in Doubt. Suppose you have a legitimate creative expense [Sec. 263A(h)], or a loss on small business stock [Sec. 1244(b)]. Most auditors don't understand these items. Trying to explain to them only confuses them and raises doubt in their minds. When in doubt, they are trained to disallow.

Whipsaw Issues. A "whipsaw" issue arises for those transactions in which the tax treatment by one party affects how the transaction should be treated by the other party. Alimony and child support are good examples. Alimony is deductible by the payer and is includible by the payee. Child support is not deductible by the payer, nor includible by the payee. Auditors disallow the tax benefits to both parties. It is then up to the auditee — now, appellant — to synchronize the treatment between the parties.

Recharacterized Items. This is that safe harbor routine for frustrated auditors. They just love to capitalize selective items, instead of allowing them to be expensed. This forces a spread-out of the deduction over many years. Whether recapitalization is proper, or whether the number of spread-out years is proper, is an appealable issue.

There is a point that we are making in all of the above. There are indeed legitimate reasons for appealing some or all of your audit results. So, don't shy away from the IRS just because you sense, or have been told, of its eternal foot-dragging when you appeal its audit changes. Do your homework; then go after the IRS.

Conference Request

Publication 5: Appeal Rights, etc., contains a section headed: *Appeals Within the Service.* This is right on point. It says, in part—

*If you decide to appeal, address your **request for a conference** to your District Director in accordance with our letter to you enclosing these instructions. Your District Director will forward your request to the Appeals Office* [of the Regional Director of Appeals], *which will arrange for a conference at a convenient time and place.*

Thus, the first thing you do is: Request a conference with an Appeals Officer. We suggest that you make the request in writing, and that you do so within about 10 days of receiving the audit change report. No particular formality is required other than your letting it be known that you do want an appeals conference. If the unagreed amount exceeds $10,000 (in tax and penalty), you will have to follow through with a formal written protest (within the 30-day period above).

In the case of a "small appeal" ($2,500 or less), or in the case of an office audit, a request for an appeals conference is all you need. But make it clear that you are *not* requesting a conference with the auditor/examiner or his supervisor. You want it with an appeals officer. You want to talk to a new face: someone who has not already prejudged you.

By making a conference request before your formal protest, you have alerted the IRS that they have an UNAGREED CASE on their hands. Upon this, the IRS has to set its processing schedule to be more mindful of the statutory tolling of your rights. This only means that your audit file will not be randomly set aside, to be handled whenever they get around to it.

Preparing Your Protest

If the unagreed amount exceeds $10,000, a written protest is required. Technically, it is only required for field audits exceeding this amount. But we think a protest should be prepared regardless of the amount, and regardless of the type of examination. Once a conference is set up, you are expected to furnish the appeals officer something in writing from which he can determine your position on the matter(s) at issue. So, you might as well prepare a written document right off the bat.

A protest requires a more structured format than a conference request. The two are not the same, though they can be combined. A conference request is simply that: a request. It is basically a notice that you intend to appeal. If your case is complicated, you may even ask for an extension of the 30-day response time for the formal protest.

A formal protest must contain certain specific information so as to constitute an evidential document of its own. Because of its evidential role, the matters in the protest must be weighed and considered (by the appeals officer). Protest matters cannot be waived aside or ignored, as so often happens with the tax examiner and revenue agents.

A written protest is structured into four general parts, namely:

A. Reference-type information: for filing purposes, taxpayer identity, and tax year(s).
B. Main body: consisting of four specific paragraphs (described below).
C. Attachments and exhibits: documents which more or less speak for themselves.
D. Perjury declaration(s): to assure that the main body statements are factual and pertinent.

There exists no official protest form. Consequently a suggested format is presented in Figure 7.2. The case reference information goes in the upper right-hand corner for taxpayer identification purposes. To make it clear that you are protesting unagreed matters resulting from the examination of your return(s), we think bold headliner words are appropriate: PROTEST: UNAGREED MATTERS.

The main body of your protest letter consists of four paragraphs as indicated in Figure 7.2. The first paragraph is a restatement of your request for an appeals conference. The second paragraph outlines the matter(s) on which you disagree with the auditor. If you can, make cross-references to the explanations on the examiner's change report. In the third paragraph, stress those facts important to your position which the examiner has sidetracked or ignored. The fourth paragraph is a "law and analysis" approach in which you try to rationalize within the context of the Internal Revenue Code. You don't have to be a tax expert on this, but you

Date:_____

Phone No.:_____

District Director
Internal Revenue Service
_____
_____

Name:_____
Address:_____
SSN:_____
Form(s):_____
Year(s):_____

PROTEST:
UNAGREED MATTER(S)

Subject:_____
Dated:_____
Symbols:_____

1 . Request is made for conference with the Appeals Office to discuss unagreed matters arising from examination of the income tax return(s) referenced above.

2 . The unagreed matters for discussion are:

(a) _____
(b) _____
(c) _____

3 . The facts pertinent to this protest are:

(a) _____
(b) _____
(c) _____

4 . The applicable law and its relevance to this protest are:

(a) _____
(b) _____
(c) _____

● Attachments
(1) _ _ _ _ _ _
(2) _ _ _ _ _ _
(3) _ _ _ _ _ _

/s/ _____
Taxpayer(s)

■ Under penalties of perjury, I declare that -

/s/ _____
Taxpayer(s)

■ Under penalties of perjury, I declare that -

/s/ _____
Protest Preparer

Fig. 7.2 - Suggested Format for Protest and Appeal Letter

might want to do a little research, or have a tax professional do it for you. Try to cite at least one tax law or tax regulation.

Each paragraph should be as succinct as possible, and not wander into emotional matters and criticisms of the examiner. IRS persons are a vindictive bunch. They want to criticize and threaten you, but they can't take any criticism themselves. Criticizing the IRS in an appeals protest probably does more harm than good.

Attachments to the protest should be those documents and portions of the tax return which you want the appeals officer to see first-hand. Unfortunately, tax examiners get to see your protest letter before the appeals officer does. This gives the examiners opportunity to "doctor up" the official file on your case, to counter your protestive points.

Specific Protest Example

To give you an idea of the type of protest specificity desired, let us cite a real-life example. The taxpayer had a small advertising business preparing market surveys and computer graphics for commercial clients. He bought a 4,000 sq. ft. commercial building (costing $365,000) and moved his staff, furniture, equipment, and files into it. Upon doing so, he paid a contractor $7,236 for various repairs and fix-ups. The examiner recharacterized these expenditures as improvements to the building and required that the $7,236 be depreciated over 30 years. And, of course, the examiner added the 20% negligence penalty. Paragraphs 2, 3, and 4 of the protest read as follows—

2. The unagreed matters for discussion are:
   (a) Whether $7,236 expensed as repairs on Schedule C should be recharacterized as capital improvements, pursuant to page 3 of the audit change report.
   (b) Whether the penalty for negligence should apply, pursuant to page 4 of the audit change report.

3. The facts pertinent to this protest are:
   (a) The following activities comprised the $7,236 expenses as repairs—
   (1) restoration to operating condition two toilets, a utility sink, and their associated

plumbing $1,068
(2) patching and repainting equipment room
for cameras and copiers............................1,150
(3) converting electrical outlets in main work
space to accommodate client-dedicated
computer workstations.............................. 896
(4) changing locks on all doors and windows,
and refitting hardware thereto....................... 972
(5) removing and replacing worn and torn
carpeting in 4 offices comprising about 1,860
sq. ft.; the building is 25 years old...............3,150

(b) The following facts relate to the building itself—
(1) the building was purchased for $365,000
(exclusive of land) and was entered on taxpayer's
depreciation schedule as recoverable over 30 years.
(2) the expenditures classed as repairs constitute less
than 2% of the total building cost [7,236 ÷ 365,000
= 0.0198].
(3) the carpet replacement represents less than 50%
of the total floor space of the building [1,860 ÷
4,000 = 0.4650].

4. The applicable law and its relevance to this protest are:
(a) Treas. Reg. 1.263(a)-1(b) says that: *Amounts paid
for incidental repairs and maintenance of property are
not capital expenditures.* Compared to $365,000, the
above items comprising the $7,236 in expenditures
are truly "incidental repairs and maintenance." They
will not "substantially prolong" the 30-year useful
life of the building.
(b) The doctrine of *de minimis exception*, as espoused in
Treas. Reg. 1.263A-1T(b)(3)(iii)(A)(2), excludes
capitalizing those expenditures which are
insubstantial and *do not result in a significantly
disproportionate allocation of costs.* The term "de
minimis" is generally construed to mean less than 5%
of the primary related-asset costs.
(c) IRC Sec. 6664(c) provides a reasonable cause
exception to the negligence penalty where the
taxpayer has acted in good faith. Furthermore,
Treas. Reg. 1.6662-3(b)(1) and (b)(2) lists eight

specific criteria of negligence, **none of which** the auditor designated in his report.

Refrain from trying to rationalize or argue your case at this point. Any discussion and rationalization of the facts and law is what the appeals conference is all about. Therefore, make your protest points as succinct as possible. Don't try to be persuasive. Just state the facts.

Acknowledgment by Appeals

Your written protest is addressed to the IRS District Director in your geographic area. The instructions tell you to mail it to the examiner who prepared your change report. Said examiner will prepare a supplemental report, countering your version of the facts with those of his own. Then, an *unagreed case file* is prepared (by the Examination Division) and forwarded to the Appeals Division.

Within six months thereafter, you will receive an official acknowledgment of your protest by an IRS Appeals Officer. You will be told that your case has been referred to him for consideration. He will provide his name and phone number, and will actually sign the acknowledgment himself. From this point on, contact is person-to-person rather than from you to a computer, and a computer to you.

Different acknowledgment forms are used, depending on the nature of each case, and on the IRS office where the conference will be held. The general thrust is in the opening paragraph which characteristically reads—

*The income tax deficiencies proposed by the District Director's Examination Division have been referred to the Appeals Office for our consideration. We would like to explore with you the possibilities of reaching a settlement without trial. I believe a **conference**, during which we could fully discuss the issues, would be mutually helpful. The conference will be informal.*

Don't get your hopes up too high. This acknowledgment wording is simply an approved formality, to say that you have one more chance before a more formal "deficiency notice" is issued to you. This is what is meant by: *the possibilities of . . . settlement without trial.* Once the IRS issues a legal Notice of Deficiency, you either pay or petition the U.S. Tax Court.

The acknowledgment letter goes on to say that—

You may present facts, arguments, and legal authority to support your position. If you plan to introduce new evidence or information, please send it to me at least five days before the conference. Please call within 10 days [of the date above] *to arrange a mutually convenient appointment.*

Be Wary of Forms 872

If your appeals conference is scheduled to be heard anytime within six months of the statute of limitations for assessing additional tax against you, you'll be asked to sign Form 872 or Form 872-A. Form 872 is titled: *Consent to Extend Time to Assess Income Tax.* Form 872-A is titled: *Special Consent to Extend the Time to Assess Tax.* Both forms are called: "waivers." That is, they waive your statutory rights and give the IRS more time to add tax, penalties, and interest to your deficiency account.

Ordinarily, when you file your return on time, the IRS has just three years to determine whether additional tax is due from you. After three years, it's too late [Sec. 6501(a)].

Consequently, when you have protested an audit change, and you've requested an appeals conference, you are starting to bump up against the statute of limitations. If your conference is scheduled more than two and one-half years after the due date of your return, the IRS will press you to sign a waiver form. It does this by sending you filled-in Form 872 or 872-A. We have some sage comments for you on this.

Form 872 has a specific **expiration date** filled in on it. That is, it is a limited time waiver. The waiver of your right to limit the assessment of additional tax expires on the date indicated on the IRS-prepared form. When you are sent this form, be sure to look for its expiration date. If it is 12 months **or less** after the statutory assessment date, go ahead and sign it. If it is more than 12 months, DO NOT SIGN IT.

On average, it takes about six months after your appeals conference to wrap up and settle the case, if it can be settled at all. Therefore, there is just no reason to allow the IRS more than 12 months to handle your appeal.

Form 872-A differs dramatically — and dangerously — from Form 872. It is **open ended**. That is, it has no expiration date! You waive your rights indefinitely, or until you gain presence of mind to obtain and file Form 872-T: Notice of Termination of Special Consent.

Our advice is: If the IRS sends you a filled-in Form 872-A, DO NOT SIGN IT. Form 872-A generally signifies that the IRS is contemplating malice towards you. The likelihood is that it is considering asserting fraud, willful evasion, or some criminal misconduct on your part. Form 872-A is used to keep you in the dark, until the IRS has built its case against you.

Appearance at Conference

An appeals conference is **not** a bargaining session. It is a good-faith effort to resolve legitimate disputes where there are grey areas in fact or where there are ambiguities in law. It is not a matter of negotiation, compromise, "splitting the differences," etc.

The conferencing objective is to determine whether you come within the applicable law or regulation, as interpreted by the IRS. The IRS is a biased agency: biased towards maximum revenue. Nevertheless, the burden of proof is on you to establish that the IRS is wrong. That is, you must overcome its presumption of correctness that we depicted back in Figure 1.1 (on page 1-6).

You have to do some preparatory homework. This means digging up the documents that you used, or should have used, when preparing your return. If it is a key document, you have to dissect it, line by line, word for word, dollar for dollar, to extract its true meaning in your favor. You may also have to do a little tax law research on point. You need to get the "flavor" of the legislative intent. You'll probably need some professional help in this regard. You want to be reasonably conversant with the applicable law on which you are relying. Don't expect — and don't ask — for any help from the appeals officer. He (or she) is not the least bit interested in settling the case in your favor. The process is more of a time extension for favoring the IRS.

Most appeals conferences do not take place until about four or five months before the extension date you signed on Form 872. And, there's a good chance you will be asked to extend it further. Don't do it! If you are so approached, this is your tipoff that you are going to be "squeezed" to accept whatever terms are offered.

A "conference" does not necessarily mean that you have to appear before the appeals officer in person. There are certain matters you can handle by phone; others you can handle by mail. Going in person — with or without a tax professional — is

Form 870	CLOSING AGREEMENT & WAIVER (Edited Title)	Date received by IRS_____
IRS File No. ___	Your Name & Address	Soc. Sec. No. ___

INCREASE / DECREASE IN TAX AND PENALTIES

Year(s)	Item	Tax	Penalty 1	Penalty 2	Etc.	Refund
TOTALS						

Explanation(s)

> **Note: 1.** "Increase / Decrease" is relative to that on the Examination Change Report.
> **2.** "Decrease" is signified by < >.
> **3.** "Refund" results from an over-assessment in tax.

Consent to Assessment and Collection

See Text

▶	/s/ Taxpayer	(date)
▶	/s/ Spouse	" "
▶	/s/ Representative	" "

Fig. 7.3 - Closing Agreement for Nontrial Appeals Case

definitely advantageous where a crucial document has to be explained and deciphered. Often, the outcome rests on a "judgment call," rather than on any proof-positive clarity of your position.

Closing Procedures

Most IRS appeals conferences are disappointing. You get your hopes up that maybe you will win a point or two. Rarely do you attain the satisfaction you seek. Appealing within the IRS is more of a PR (public relations) charade. Its only positive advantage is that it forces you to review your position thoroughly and decide whether you want to press on into Tax Court. If you do go to Tax Court, one of the prerequisities is that you've gone through the appeals process.

For nontrial cases, the closing procedure is rather simple. Form 870 is used. This form is titled: *Waiver of Restrictions on Assessment and Collection of Deficiency in Tax and Acceptance of Overassessment.* This title is quite a mouthful. The idea is that if you agree to the settlement terms — additional tax, reduced penalty, some overassessment (refund) — you have to allow the IRS additional time to go through its billing/refunding process and its computation of statutory interest therewith. An edited and abridged arrangement of Form 870 is presented in Figure 7.3. Although prepared by the Appeals Office, it is not signed by that office.

If you intend to close the case, do so by signing Form 870, as submitted. The IRS needs at least 90 days to complete its processing of the case, before any Form 872 that you have signed expires. If this expiration date is too tight for the IRS, expect to receive, by Certified Mail, a statutory NOTICE OF DEFICIENCY [Sec. 6212(a)]. This notice gives you 90 days to either—

1. Pay the tax and penalty, then file for a refund.
2. Sign another Form 872, then request that the Notice of Deficiency be rescinded.
3. Petition the U.S. Tax Court to stay the IRS's assessment and collection actions.

8

SMALL TAX COURT

When The Amount Of Tax (And Penalty) "Placed In Dispute" Is $10,000 Or Less, Special Procedures Apply. These Are Elective Under Section 7463, Following A NOTICE OF DEFICIENCY From The IRS. You Have 90 Days From Said Notice To Request And File A SMALL TAX PETITION With The U.S. Tax Court. There Follows A "Conference Exchange" Of Information And Documents Between You And The IRS That Often Leads To Settlement Without Trial. Upon "Calendar Call" For Trial, Informal Rules Of Evidence Apply. A Small Tax Court Decision Cannot Be Appealed By You Nor By The IRS.

Paying taxes is such a pain these days. Family, personal, financial, and other setbacks induce procrastination in filing returns and paying "those damn taxes." This is a burden that all governments (federal, state, local) impose for the privilege of living and breathing.

There is also bureaucratic nit-picking and stonewalling to contend with, when there is some dispute as to the amount of correct tax. Tax agencies and agents are not known for their patience and empathy towards taxpayers with valid complaints.

The result is that there is a growing body of disgruntled taxpayers out there. In some cases, there are good reasons for the disgruntlement; in other cases, there are not good reasons.

More and more, the IRS is resorting to the use of pay-or-go-to-court demand letters. Officially, each such letter is called: Notice of

Deficiency. Such a letter gives you the option of paying the tax now, or going into Tax Court. If you don't petition the court within the time specified, the IRS will assess the tax. Once this is done, it has authority to levy your wages and bank accounts or to place tax liens against your property.

Once you are pushed up against the wall to pay-or-go-to-court, there are some legalities to contend with. The principal legality is the filing of a formal petition with the U.S. Tax Court. However, if it is a "small tax case," the subsequent legalities are rather *informal* to the point where no attorney is needed.

The Small Tax Court informalities are sanctioned by Section 7463 of the IR Code. Consequently, our focus in this chapter is to familiarize you with the Section 7463 procedures. We do this for those situations where you have bona fide reasons for disputing a tax deficiency. But you have to do some homework, and prepare your case diligently.

"Small Tax" Defined

A small tax case (before the U.S. Tax Court) is one in which the amount of deficiency in dispute (including penalties and other amounts) totals $10,000 or less. This ceiling amount applies to any one taxable year, or any one taxable period (if less than a year).

If there are three tax disputive years, for example, two of which are each under $10,000 and one over $10,000, you then have two separate small tax cases, and one large tax case.

If the large tax case is $12,500, for example, and you are willing to concede and pay $2,500 of that amount, the *amount placed in dispute* (official words) is $10,000. You can still use the small tax case procedures.

The applicable law on point is Section 7463. Its official heading is: *Disputes Involving $10,000 Or Less*. Note that this heading does not say "deficiencies" of $10,000 or less. It is the amount of dispute, *not* the amount of deficiency, that triggers the informal procedures in Small Tax Court.

Subsection 7463(a): In General, says in part—

In the case of any petition filed with the Tax Court for a redetermination of a deficiency where neither the amount of the deficiency placed in dispute, nor the amount of any claimed overpayment, exceeds $10,000 for any one taxable *year. . . [then]* ***at the option of the taxpayer*** *. . .* [Emphasis added.]

Particularly note this last clause: "at the option of the taxpayer." This means that you have to specifically request that the informal procedures apply. Doing so, you give up your subsequent appeal rights, but you can save time and professional fees. If you have a good case and prepare it well, you probably can do as well as most professionals anyhow.

Eligibility for informal procedures is not a function of one's gross income. It is simply a matter of the amount of tax in dispute, for each tax period. Each tax period is addressed separately, even though there may be several tax periods sequentially involved. Also, one should note that there is some movement in Congress to increase the "small" amount from $10,000 to (perhaps) $25,000.

Notice of Deficiency

A Notice of Deficiency is a formal demand for payment. Its purpose is to flash at you the IRS-asserted deficiency in tax and its associated penalty or penalties, if any. You are expected to pay the amount(s) shown, or pursue the options permitted. The notice is sent by certified mail [Sec. 6212(a)].

In most cases, before the formal notice is sent to you, you have been computer contacted by the IRS at least once, and, in some cases, twice. In rare cases, where you have responded plausibly to the first or second contact, you may be computer contacted a third time. Thus, you will have had adequate forewarning as to the amount of tax in question, the year (or period) to which it applies, and the general nature of the IRS's assertions. You may not agree, but at least you know that you are on the IRS's watchlist.

A notice of deficiency is a preprinted letter-type form, along the lines illustrated in Figure 8.1. The same letter form is sent to all deficiency addressees, whether they are small tax or large tax in amount. There are six paragraphs in the letter; you select the one that meets your choice of options . . . then respond.

For small tax petitions, the pertinent paragraph says—

If you dispute not more than $10,000 for any one tax year, a simplified procedure is provided by the Tax Court for small tax

Internal Revenue Service Department of the Treasury	Social Security Number Tax Year_____ Deficiency_____ Penalty 1 $_____ Penalty 2 $_____ Penalty 3 $_____
Date _____ Certified Mail Adressee _____ _____ _____	Person to Contact _____ _____

Dear Taxpayer:

1.	NOTICE OF DEFICIENCY & enclosed statement
2.	90 DAYS (or 150 DAYS if outside U.S.) _____ To Contest, MUST PETITION U.S. Tax Court_____ Instructions for signing petition_____
3.	Instructions: Small tax cases_____
4.	If no petition, sign waiver_____
5.	If no waiver, will assess _____
6.	If questions, phone or write_____

Enclosures   Commissioner, IRS

● Statement   by _____ /s/ _____

● Waiver   _____ name _____

                        _____ title _____

Fig. 8.1 - General Format & Contents: Notice of Deficiency

cases. You may obtain information about this procedure, as well as a petition form you can use, by writing to the Clerk of the United States Tax Court at 400 Second Street N.W., Washington, D.C. 20217. You should do this promptly if you intend to file a petition with the Tax Court.

This is pretty clear. You have to write to Washington, D.C. for a petition form. In several weeks' time, you'll receive a petition form in the mail, together with a little pamphlet of instructions entitled: *Election of Small Tax Case Procedure & Preparation of Petitions*. The instructions tell you that you must file your petition not later than 90 days after **the date on** the notice of deficiency mailed to you. (150 days if the notice is addressed to a person outside the U.S.) They further say—

*Please note that the period is 90 days and **not** 3 months.*

This is also a way of telling you that NO EXTENSIONS ARE PERMITTED. None whatsoever.

The IRS letter notice also tells you about the 90 days. In addition, the 90-day letter says—

If you have any questions about this letter, please write to the person whose name and address are shown above, or you may call that person at the number shown above.

You can write or phone if you want to, but don't expect any concessions on the deficiency amount. The IRS has its time gun at your head. So don't burn up your time needlessly. Knuckle down and prepare to file your petition.

The Petition Format

When you write to the Clerk of the Tax Court (Washington, D.C.), be sure to ask for T.C. Form 2: *Petition: Small Tax Case*. This form is quite simplified and is essentially self-explanatory. The key dollar amount entries are:

☐ Amount of deficiency disputed
☐ Penalty, if any, disputed
☐ Amount of overpayment claimed

You make separate entries for each year (or period) to which the notice — or notices — of deficiency relate(s). It is possible that the same disputive issues apply to two or more consecutive years.

An edited and abbreviated T.C. Form 2 appears as illustrated in Figure 8.2. As you can see, it consists of four paragraphs plus an

```
........................................          ........................................
:      Petitioner(s)          :          :    Space for Official   :
:    Address & Phone No.      :          :    Stamp of the Court    :
........................................          ........................................
```

UNITED STATES TAX COURT

```
......................................................  )
         Petitioner(s)           )
              v.                 )
Commissioner of Internal Revenue, )   DOCKET NO. _____
          Respondent             )
_____ )
```

PETITION

1. Petitioner(s) disagree(s) with the tax deficiency(ies) for the year(s) _____ as set forth in the NOTICE OF DEFICIENCY dated _____ , A COPY OF WHICH IS ATTACHED. The notice was issued by the Office of the Internal Revenue Service at _____ .

2. Petitioner(s) taxpayer identification (social security) number(s) is (are) _____

3. Petitioner(s) dispute(s) the following:

Year	Amount of Deficiency Disputed	Addition to Tax (Penalty) if any , Disputed	Amount of Over- payment Claimed
____	_____	_____	_____
____	_____	_____	_____
____	_____	_____	_____

4. Set forth those adjustments, i.e. changes, in the NOTICE OF DEFICIENCY with which you disagree and why you disagree.
    _____
    _____
    _____

Petitioner(s) request(s) that this case be conducted under the "small tax case" procedures . . . *

/s/
_____   _____
PETITIONER   DATE   ADDRESS & PHONE NO.
/s/
_____   _____
PETITIONER (SPOUSE) DATE   ADDRESS & PHONE NO.

* If you do not want to make this request, place an "X" here. [   ]

Fig. 8.2 - General Format & Contents: Small Tax Petition

election request at the very end. For space reasons, we do not show all of the election request in Figure 8.2. However, we cite it in full below.

The "election" is so-called because you have to expressly request small tax procedures. Such procedures do not automatically apply simply because the total amount placed in dispute for any one year (or period) is $10,000 or less.

The election request reads in full as follows:

Petitioner(s) request(s) that this case be conducted under the "small tax case" procedures authorized by Congress to provide the taxpayer(s) with an informal, prompt, and inexpensive hearing at a reasonably convenient location. Consistent with these objectives, a decision in a "small tax case" is final and cannot be appealed to higher Courts (the Court of Appeals and the Supreme Court) by the Internal Revenue Service or the Petitioner(s). If you do not want to make this request, you should place an "X" in the following box. ☐

It should be evident, now, why you have to expressly elect small tax procedures. Any decision on the case is final. Said decision is not appealable by you nor by the IRS. Furthermore, you cannot use a decision in your favor as the precedent for similar issues in subsequent years. A decision applies only to the one designated year.

Offsetting the downside to small tax decisions is the fact that the procedures are informal, no attorney is required in your behalf, and, except in quite unusual cases, no actual appearance at court trial is involved. Even so, a written decision is rendered and entered into court records like any regular Tax Court trial.

Paragraph 4 Examples

The principal focus in a small tax petition is paragraph 4 (in Figure 8.2). This is where the petitioner sets forth his reasons why he thinks he is right, and the IRS wrong. Paragraph 4 essentially makes or breaks a case.

Keep the paragraph 4 items objective. State your facts clearly, and point to specific errors that you believe the IRS made. Stick to the key points supporting your position. Don't stray off into vehement criticisms of the IRS nor of the tax system in general. A small tax petition is not a forum for registering your general dissatisfaction with taxes.

On the official petition form, paragraph 4 is assigned eight full spreadlines. Each line affords ample space for handprinting what you want to say. If you type, you can get the equivalent of two typewritten lines for each form-provided line.

Do not write pages and pages of reasons and explanations. Limit yourself to the eight lines only. Don't worry, you'll be given opportunity later to furnish all of the explanatory depth and evidential documentation that you wish. The contents on the eight lines serve primarily for cataloging the nature of your case, and for assigning it to a hearing officer. Rarely do the contents in a petition provide all information needed for decision making.

With the above in mind, we relate three separate examples of how you might prepare your own entries on paragraph 4:

Example 1 — A high school teacher retired in 1985 for medical reasons. She underwent major surgery and extended convalescence. She filed her return several years late. In 1990, she received a notice of deficiency for $7,827; penalty #1 for $829; penalty #2 for $391; and penalty #3 for $125. Total amount = $9,172.

Paragraph 4 of the teacher's petition read (as edited)—

I filed my 1985 return late (with medical explanations attached thereto). I paid an additional tax of $2,009. Yet, the IRS claims I owe another $7,827. My withholdings alone were $4,513. Furthermore, I am entitled to a refund of $2,975 arising from the 3-year rule for nontaxability while recovering my contribution to the state teachers' retirement system.

Example 2 — A 7.1 earthquake damaged the home of a contractor and his wife in 1989, along with thousands of other homes in the area. The damage occurred on October 17, 1989. Within days, after calling more than 10 property appraisers, taxpayers obtained an oral estimate of $15,000 from a reputable appraiser. He would not provide a written appraisal because he was too busy with other damage appraisals exceeding $300,000. Taxpayers used the $15,000 and filed Form 4684 (Casualty Loss) with their regular return. The return was audited. There was agreement on other matters, but not on the casualty loss. After other appeals, the taxpayers received in 1991 a notice of deficiency for $2,791 plus a negligence penalty of $558. Total amount = $3,349.

Paragraph 4 of the contractor's petition read (as edited)—

The original estimate of $15,000 was obtained immediately after the damage on October 17, 1989. On April 4, 1991 photographs were shown to the auditor indicating a higher amount. Yet, the auditor insisted on a written estimate. This came in at $7,278 on June 17, 1991: almost two years later. In the interim, we had done all the cleanup and the nonstructural repairs ourselves. The original estimate was conservative and should have been allowed in full.

Example 3 — A self-employed language translator's 1985 return was audited in 1988. She had a complex Schedule C (Small Business) return consisting of some 1,650 separate entries. All were fully documented. The auditor spent 18 hours (over eight months' time) on his examination. Because he found nothing of substance to disallow, he recharacterized $12,062 of small tools and computer software as depreciable items (rather than currently expensable). He required their deduction over seven years. He then asserted a negligence penalty of $203, which the taxpayer appealed and reappealed. Subsequently, in 1990 she received a notice of deficiency for the $203 penalty.

Paragraph 4 of translator's petition read (as edited)—

The auditor spent 8 months on my return. I pleaded with his supervisor beforehand that it was a repeat audit of my 1984 return, for which there was no change. He picked and dawdled (causing me to cancel several of my business appointments) just to contrive some adjustment for his IRS computer training program. He cannot justify a negligence penalty against me; I can against him.

P.S. The $203 penalty was cancelled shortly after the petition was filed.

Filing Fee, Copies, Etc.

The U.S. Tax Court is NOT part of the Internal Revenue Service. It is a "sister agency" to the IRS, but it is an independent branch of government of its own. As such, when a petition is filed with the Tax Court, a nominal filing fee is required. The current fee is $60 . . . payable to "Clerk, U.S. Tax Court."

The address of the Tax Court in Washington, D.C. is in the notice of deficiency which the IRS sent to you. Send your original petition and two copies of it to that address. **Do not send it** back to the IRS's address on the notice. The IRS may not forward it to the Tax Court for you. Keep in mind that there are two separate bureaucracies involved. It is for this reason that to the original petition, and to each separate copy thereof, you attach a complete copy of the notice of deficiency. Do not attach anything else to the petition.

Though not directly attached to the petition, you are also required to sign and send an original and two copies of T.C. Form 4: Designation of Place of Trial (City and State). When you request petition Form 2, the clerk will also send you Form 4. In the instructions therewith is a listing of some 80 cities throughout the U.S. where small tax cases may be heard. You designate the city most convenient for you. You may not actually go to trial there, but all of the paperwork will be handled through that office.

It is advisable to file your Small Tax Court petition by certified mail. This way you have proof positive of your date of mailing. A certified mail receipt from the U.S. postal system fulfills the legal filing requirement.

When the court clerk in Washington, D.C. receives your petition (Form 2), city designation (Form 4), **and** the $60 filing fee, you'll receive back a *Notification of Receipt of Petition*. This receipt will assign you a docket number, such as: Docket No. 8315-98S. The "S" means small tax case; the "98" is the year docketed; and the "8315" is the consecutive number of such petitions received for that year. You are instructed to use this docket number on all letters and documents that you prepare on your case.

Once a docket number is assigned to your petition, your disputive issue is solely within the jurisdiction of the Tax Court. While under its jurisdiction, the IRS cannot make further demands on you regarding that issue. Matters are taken out of IRS hands until a written decision from the Tax Court is rendered.

May Represent Yourself

The great majority of small tax petitions never actually go to trial. We'll exemplify this shortly below. But if your case does go to trial, or even if it doesn't, you can represent yourself all along the way. No attorney is really needed. The self-representation is very similar to small claims court or traffic court procedures in many cities of the U.S.

The instructions that accompany petition Form 2 say, in part—

Most petitioners in small tax cases represent themselves. The trial will be conducted in an orderly manner, as simply as possible. Any evidence you offer which the Court thinks will have value as proof of your claim will be admissible.

If you have receipts or other papers or documents which support your claim, you should bring them with you when you come to Court for trial. The Court will try to help you develop the facts in your case through your testimony and that of other witnesses, and any receipts, papers, or documents which you bring with you to the trial.

We want to especially caution you about one important matter. Any papers, documents, or statements that you may have given to the IRS, either before or after your petition is filed, are NOT AVAILABLE to the Tax Court. You'll understand this better if you keep in mind at all times that the IRS and Tax Court are different jurisdictional authorities. The IRS has no obligation whatsoever to turn over to the Tax Court any of your papers, documents, or statements. In adversarial reality, the IRS goes out of its way to withhold from, and deny to, the Court any information that it has in your favor.

Consequently, the full burden is on your shoulders to make photocopies of whatever information you have given to the IRS that is helpful in supporting your case. You cannot count on the IRS to be of any help (assuming that it ever was). Keep always in mind that the IRS is your adversary: not your friend. You may get limited help from the Court itself, but don't count on the trial coordinator holding your hand and guiding you through. If you need handholding, you probably would not have had the spunk to file a petition in the first place.

Events After Filing

As stated above, when your petition and filing fee are received by the Tax Court, a notice of receipt is sent to you. The receipt shows the docket number and the official date thereof. The receipt also says—

Petition served on respondent on __(date)__. [The "respondent" is the IRS.] All papers and correspondence MUST bear the DOCKET NUMBER given above.

Clerk of the Court

Within 60 days after service upon the IRS by the court, an IRS Appeals Officer (under the supervision of the IRS District Counsel) will send you a form printed Acknowledgment Letter. This letter reads in part as—

*Your case has been referred to our office. We will write or call you soon to arrange a mutually satisfactory date for a **conference**. If you need to contact us in the meantime, you may write to the address below or call at the telephone number above.* [Emphasis added.]

The IRS is not showing you any special courtesy by this acknowledgment letter. They are required by Tax Court rules to do it, or they lose by default. If the IRS defaults, the case would be dismissed and a decision would be entered in your favor. The IRS is not going to let this happen.

When the IRS sends the case acknowledgment to you, the Tax Court expects you to engage in a "conference" with the IRS. This is *not* a formal affair, nor is it set for any fixed time or place. It can be — and often is — a series of ongoing exchanges of information and documents by phone, mail, or personal appearance. All of this exchanging of information and opposing points of view should take place within about 90 days after the IRS acknowledgment letter is sent. This is the "feeling out" phase of the conferencing. You want to know what the IRS will give, and the IRS wants to know what you will give. This is *not* just some marketplace form of bargaining; it is a supervised testing of the legal positions of each party.

The feeling-out phase terminates abruptly when you and the IRS each receives from the Tax Court a **Notice Setting Case for Trial**. This is the formal prodding that you and the IRS have to put something specific in writing. That which is put in writing is called a *stipulation*. There are two forms of stipulations, namely: (a) Settlement Stipulation, and (b) Trial Stipulation. We'll discuss each of these stipulatory forms, separately, below.

In the meantime, we want to summarize for you your post-petition events. We do this graphically in Figure 8.3. Particularly note therein the number of days' time between the notice setting case for trial, and the actual date of trial. This time period is approximately 90 days. It is during this 90-day pretrial period that some written stipulation must be prepared.

"Calendar Call" Explained

The date set by the Tax Court for trial, in its official notice, is referred to as *calendar call*. It is referenced as this because the notice says—

The parties are hereby notified that the above-entitled case is set for trial at the Trial Session beginning on ___(date)___ . The calendar for that Session will be called at ___(hour)___ on that date and both parties are expected to be present. YOUR FAILURE TO APPEAR MAY RESULT IN DISMISSAL OF THE CASE AND ENTRY OF DECISION AGAINST YOU.

Trying to change a calendar call is next to impossible. It is a show-up-or-lose-your-case date. No excuses. No extensions.

Prior to the calendar call date, the IRS Appeals Office handling your case will write you a "final call" letter. His wording will read something like this—

We feel that it will be mutually advantageous if the issues in this case can be settled without trial. Since the time for further conferencing is short, we ask that you call us within 10 days so that we might discuss what is still needed and proceed with resolving the issue(s) prior to the trial date.

This is not saying that the IRS has conceded the case. What the IRS is saying is: "Can we settle the case without trial?" The term "settle" means you may win a little or a lot, or you may lose a little or a lot. The Tax Court defines the term "settle" as—

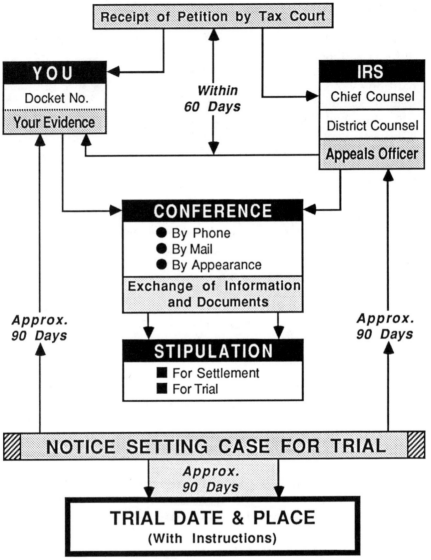

Fig.8.3 - Post-Petition Events to Settlement Pretrial

Meaning that the petitioner and respondent will agree on the amount of tax due, or that no tax is due, or that a refund is due, without a court trial. Settlement documents should be presented to the Court prior to the call of the calendar.

Settlement Stipulation

Thus, if you and the IRS can agree on a settlement without trial, that's fine with the Tax Court. If a settlement is in the offing, it must be in the form of a joint stipulation. This means that your signature and date are required alongside the signature and date of an IRS official. The IRS will prepare the stipulation and submit it to you for approval.

The IRS Appeals Officer will send you a form letter saying, in part—

We have prepared a proposed Stipulation document to be filed with the U.S. Tax Court reflecting the agreement we reached during consideration of your case. If you approve, please sign and return the original and one copy of the Stipulation in the envelope provided. After our approval, the Stipulation is forwarded to the IRS District Counsel for filing with the Tax Court. The Tax Court will notify you of entry of the Stipulation.

Earlier, we cited to you a petition plea by a retired high school teacher, which we designated as "Example 1." She filed late because of major medical reasons. In addition to asserting a deficiency against her, the IRS added a number of penalties.

As a result of her petition and the further submission of documentation, the IRS agreed that there was no net deficiency; that no penalties applied; and that, indeed, a refund in the amount of $2,898 was due her. The official Stipulation to this effect read as follows:

It is hereby stipulated that the following statement shows the petitioner's income tax liability for the taxable year at issue, which is agreed to by both parties:

Tax liability	*$3,703*
Total payments	*6,601*
Overpayment	*$2,898*

The point that we are making here is that it is possible to settle a small tax case without actually going to trial. Much, of course, depends on the right circumstances, the right documentation, and a will to challenge the IRS when it is wrong.

Stipulation for Trial

If the parties cannot settle the issue(s) before trial, then appearance at trial is mandatory. Tax Court Rule 134 provides that cases will not be continued other than under exceptional and unusual circumstances. Generally, requests by petitioners for continuance are deemed dilatory and will be denied. Rarely does the IRS request continuance because it already has the petitioner boxed in a corner. The "calendar call" is cast in concrete. This puts pressure on the petitioner more than on the IRS.

Even if there is no pretrial settlement, Tax Court Rule 91 requires that the parties enter into a written stipulation as to those material facts and documents that are not in dispute. That is, the parties are—

> *required to stipulate, to the fullest extent to which complete or qualified agreement can or fairly should be made.* [Emphasis added.]

By agreeing to those matters that you can agree upon, and by agreeing to those matters that you cannot agree upon, the Tax Court is in a better position to focus on the disagreements.

The items over which there is disagreement usually involve some fact or circumstance, or some document, or some oral or written statement that is ambiguous. It could be interpreted either way: your way or the IRS's way. It is up to you, the petitioner, to sway the court that your interpretation is the more correct.

The instructions accompanying the notice of calendar call say, in part, that—

> *The parties are responsible for presenting all evidence to the Court **at the time of trial**. The evidence consists of the stipulation of facts, sworn testimony at trial, and any documentary evidence (books and records) accepted by the Court as exhibits at the trial. . . . Information or documents previously presented to the IRS are **not** before the Court. Therefore, **at trial**, the parties must present all documents and the testimony of all witnesses that they want the Court to consider in deciding the case.* [Emphasis added.]

The court is trying to warn you that whatever information or documents you may have given the IRS before trial are of no value whatsoever unless you present them again at trial. The IRS has no obligation to bring those prior papers to the court's attention. In fact, the IRS may claim they don't exist, unless you produce them in court. The IRS is not above "tampering" with your documents that do exist.

In most small tax cases, the petitioner will be called upon to testify in his own behalf. The procedure is to be sworn, take the witness stand, and give an opening statement as to your position, and why. The court will allow the IRS to cross-examine you. After which, the court (trial judge) will ask questions of you also.

You may refute the IRS's questions, documents, and statements of its position in any way you wish. So long as your demeanor is civil and your rationale is objective, you are not held to all of the formal rules of evidence. The trial judge is trying to sort things out within the framework of applicable tax laws as he or she sees them.

Finality of Decision

Sooner, rather than later, all small tax disputes must come to an end. The is *the* key advantage of Small Tax Court proceedings. The IRS can not drag a case out endlessly . . . nor can the petitioner. The court is required by IR Code Section 7459(a) to prepare its written decision *as quickly as possible*. Often, this is within 90 days after settlement pretrial or after trial is concluded.

If trial occurred, the judge may render an oral decision. In such event, the oral decision is intended more as a way of instructing the IRS attorney when preparing the written decision for the court to sign. The decision is a concise statement of conclusions regarding the issue(s) raised in the petition.

Small Tax Court decisions are generally no more than two pages in length. Page 1 is the decision itself for the judge's signature. However, it is not signed by the judge until after page 2 has been signed and dated by the petitioner and the IRS attorney assigned to the case. Said signatures appear below two stereotyped stipulatory statements.

The two (somewhat self-explanatory) statements are—

It is hereby stipulated that the Court may enter the foregoing decision in the above-entitled case in accordance with the stipulation of the parties submitted herewith.

It is further stipulated that, effective upon the entry of this decision by the Court, petitioner waives the restriction contained in IRC Sec. 6213(a) prohibiting the assessment and collection of the deficiencies and additions to the tax (plus statutory interest) until the decision of the Tax Court has become final.

The purpose of this second stipulation is to enable the IRS to close out the case as soon as possible, without further delay.

Each decision document is of simple format. It has a preamble clause followed by ORDERED AND DECIDED THAT—

- *There is a deficiency in tax for ___(year)___ in the amount of $_____.*
- *There is no deficiency in tax for ___(year)___.*
- *There is an overpayment of tax for ___(year)___ in the amount of $_____.*
- *There is an addition to tax (penalty) due from petitioner under the provisions of IRC Sec. _____ for taxable year _____.*
- *There is no addition to tax (penalty) due from petitioner under the provisions of IRC Sec. _____ for taxable year _____.*

                                        (s)_____
                                        Judge, U.S. Tax Court

Entered: ___(date)___

Once the judge signs the decision, it is then immediately entered into the records of the court. There it becomes final. It cannot be appealed. It cannot be appealed by the petitioner, nor by the IRS. This is the understanding, or should have been the understanding, when you elected the Small Tax Court procedures.

9

LIENS, LEVIES, & SEIZURES

Collection Enforcement Starts With An Automatic Lien On All Property And Rights To Property Of A Delinquent Taxpayer, When An IRS "Assessment" Is Made. Because Of Glaring Omissions In Section 6203: Method Of Assessment, The Initial Amount Sought Is Invariably OVERASSESSED. If No Corrective Response On Your Part, A NOTICE AND DEMAND For Full Payment Is Issued, Good For 10 Years. Once Collection Begins, The Most Frequently Used Tool Is The LEVY. It Enables The IRS To Take One's Wages, Bank Accounts, And Financial Assets Without Forewarning The Delinquent Taxpayer. Distress And Destitution Often Result.

In Chapters 2 and 3, we mentioned but did not explain how *collection enforcement* really works. If allowed to proceed unchecked, the targeted taxpayer can be left emotionally distraught and financially destitute. Once a lien, levy, or seizure is in process, damage to a delinquent taxpayer is inevitable. We'll cite a true case of death by massive stroke.

Under Rights Acts 1 and 2 (described in Chapter 1), the IRS is supposed to provide reasonable opportunity to "work things out." In reality, the delinquent taxpayer is caught in a quagmire of demands, responses, more demands, and more responses. He becomes utterly confused and lapses into mental stall. When he misses some trigger date, the collection dragon barrels on.

Accordingly, we want to explain to you the IRS's authority for assessing tax and enforcing its claims against delinquent taxpayers. We all know that the bedrock function of the IRS is to assess and collect tax. To carry out its revenue-collection functions, Congress has granted to the IRS the enforcement powers of lien, levy, and seizure. At times, these can be Draconian measures.

We are not here to defend the IRS's enforcement actions, nor to recommend that you ignore them. Once you allow your tax account to become delinquent, there isn't much salvation for you. There are, however, steps you can take to minimize the agony and abate the abuses of enforcement. But these steps — your rights — are not brought to your attention willingly by IRS enforcers. You have to discover them on your own as you go along. Helping you to discover your disagreeing rights and actions with respect to collection enforcement is what this chapter is all about.

Authority to Assess

The IRS just can't go out and collect money at will, or based on whim. It can't do this, even though some of its agents and enforcers behave as though they can. The IRS must first *assess* a tax and then — after following certain statutory procedures — go out and collect it. A valid assessment is a separate precondition all of its own.

The IRS's basic authority to assess is set forth in Section 6201(a) of the Tax Code. This section reads in pertinent part as—

*The Secretary [IRS] is authorized **and required** to make the inquiries, determinations, and assessments of all taxes (including interest, additional amounts, additions to tax, and assessable penalties) imposed by this [Code] . . . in the manner provided by law. Such authority shall extend to and include . . . all taxes determined by the taxpayer or by the [IRS] as to which returns or lists are made.* [Emphasis added.]

As you can surmise from the emphasized portions, an assessment has to be made based upon some amount of tax shown or not shown on a tax return. The preferable return is that which is made voluntarily by the taxpayer. But, if no return is made by the taxpayer when required, a return is made by the IRS for that taxpayer [Sec. 6020(b): *Authority to Execute Returns*]. It also should be pointed out that the IRS can assess against a minor child (who receives tax accountable income) by assessing the parent of that child [Sec. 6201(c)].

Assessments also can be made for unpaid taxes, erroneous credits, computational errors, excessive claims (for refunds), employment tax, death taxes, gift taxes, excise taxes (on luxury items and energy sources) and so on.

As the statutory words above indicate, the IRS is required only to make **an** assessment. It is not required to make a correct assessment. The IRS can — and does intentionally — make *erroneous* assessments. Part of this is due to haste; part is due to laziness; and part is due to the arrogance of power.

Overassessing Is the Norm

The methodology for assessing a taxpayer is an internal affair of the IRS. The procedures that it uses are not subject to public scrutiny in any way. This could be the explanation for its habitual overassessing. As one IRS Assessment Officer recently admitted to the author herein: "We always overassess; that's the nature of our business."

Overassessing is silently authorized by the succinct wording of Section 6203: *Method of Assessment.* It is a two-sentence statute. The first sentence reads in full as—

The assessment shall be made by recording the liability of the taxpayer in the office of the [IRS] *in accordance with rules or regulations prescribed by* [itself].

Do you see anything in this sentence about the assessment being true, correct, and complete? Do you see anything about the assessment being prepared under "penalties of perjury"? Of course you don't. As a taxpayer, you have to make such a certification yourself, but NOT the IRS! Now you know why IRS assessments are rarely reliable.

The second sentence of Section 6203 reads in full as—

Upon request of the taxpayer, the [IRS] *shall furnish the taxpayer a copy of the record of assessment.*

In other words, because the IRS overassesses, it is up to the taxpayer to request his assessment record and make a correct determination himself. There is no self-policing within the IRS for doing so. This is the taproot behind all of the horror stories you may have heard about the IRS's collection enforcement procedures.

Regulation 301.6203-1 expands a bit on Section 6203. In pertinent part, this regulation reads—

> *The assessment shall be made by an assessment officer signing the summary record of assessment. The summary record,* **through supporting records,** *shall provide identification of the taxpayer, the character of the liability, the taxable period, and the amount of the assessment. . . . The date of the assessment is the date the summary record is signed by an assessment officer. If the taxpayer requests a copy of the record of assessment, he shall be furnished a copy of the* **pertinent parts** *of the assessment.* [Emphasis added.]

Apparently, when you request a copy of your assessment record, you are only given the "pertinent parts." You are not given the supporting records. What this means is that the pertinent parts comprise the *gross income* side of the assessment computation. Your deductions, expenses, credits, and basis in assets sold are irrelevant to the assessment process. The IRS wants to inflict maximum pain for extracting maximum dollars from you.

The Collections Dragon

The shortest tax law of all is IRC Section 6301: *Collection Authority*. It consists of exactly 12 words, namely:

> *The* [IRS] *shall collect the taxes imposed by the internal revenue laws.*

That's it! There are no subsections, no exceptions, and no provisos. The tax assessed shall be collected . . . and it **will** be collected . . . one way or another.

There are some limitations placed on the IRS. The rules on this are set forth in Section 6501: *Limitations on Assessment and Collection*. There are 15 subsections, (a) through (o), wherein assessment and collection shall not be authorized. The idea is to prescribe certain statutory times after which a taxpayer can rest in peace. The "rest in peace" applies to only one year at a time.

Of the 15 limitation rules, the most common are as follows:

Assessment (and collection) must begin—
(1) within 3 years after the prescribed date of a return
— whether filed before, on, or after this date.
(2) within 6 years after the prescribed date
— when 25% or more of gross income is omitted.
(3) whenever the IRS gets around to it ("open years")
— for no returns, false returns, or fraudulent returns
(4) no later than the time agreed to by mutual agreement
between taxpayer and the IRS.

Once proper assessment has been made, the IRS has **10 years** to collect it. This is so prescribed by Section 6502(a), namely:

*Such tax may be collected by levy or by a proceeding in court, but only if the levy is made or the proceeding begun . . . **within 10 years** after assessment of the tax.*

The term "levy" is generic for liens, levies, and seizures. The term "proceeding in court" means any court proceeding where there is dispute over the legality of a lien, levy, or seizure.

As an instructional summary, we present in Figure 9.1 a general overview of the collection process. We suggest that you study Figure 9.1 carefully. It gives you a road map of what to expect from the IRS, as its enforcement process barrels along.

Notice and Demand: 10 Days

Technically, collection begins the moment an assessment officer signs an entry in the official records of the IRS. Legally, it does not begin until the targeted taxpayer is served NOTICE AND DEMAND. The "demand" part means full payment of the unpaid tax *within 10 days.*

The requirement for serving legal notice and demand is spelled out in Section 6303(a): ***Notice and Demand for Tax.*** The pertinent portions read—

*The [IRS] shall . . . within 60 days, after the making of an assessment of a tax pursuant to section 6203 [method of assessment], give notice to **each person liable** for the unpaid tax, stating the amount and demanding payment thereof. Such notice shall be left at the dwelling or usual place of business of*

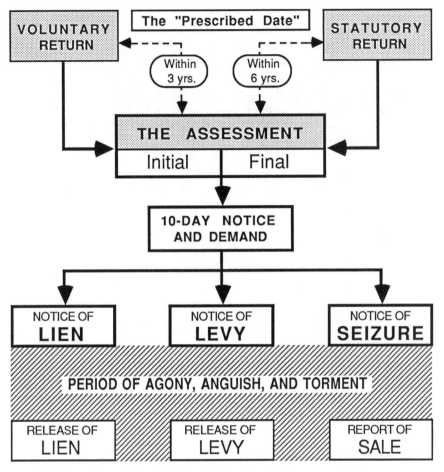

Fig.9.1 - Overview of the Collection Enforcement Process

*such person, or shall be sent by mail to such person's **last known address**.* [Emphasis added.]

Once the notice has been legally served, the specified amount is due and payable. The amount may be — will be — dead wrong. But, at this point, it is too late to correct any errors or overassessments. You had your chance earlier. Even if the amount is egregiously wrong, you still have to pay (or arrange to pay) the amount demanded. It is only *after* the demanded amount is paid that you can address its errors and overassessments.

What happens if the demand notice is sent to an old address? Answer: It is still a legal notice if you have not changed the old address on your latest filings with the IRS.

How a Lien Works

Of the three Draconian enforcement measures, a Federal Tax Lien is probably the least obnoxious. A *lien* is a security interest by the IRS in all property and rights to property of the delinquent taxpayer. It *clouds title* to property, thereby preventing it from being sold, transferred, or further encumbered. A formal Notice of Lien is prepared primarily in those situations where the delinquent is "cash poor and property rich" — relatively speaking.

Technically, a lien attaches automatically where a 10-day notice and demand have been served, and the taxpayer — for whatever reason — does not or cannot pay. This automaticity is by *operation of law* as set forth in Tax Code Section 6321: *Lien for Taxes.*

Section 6321 is one paragraph in length. The words themselves exemplify the old adage that: "The power to tax is the power to destroy." The paragraph reads in full as—

If any person liable to pay any tax neglects or refuses to pay the same after demand, the amount (including any interest, additional amount, addition to tax, or assessable penalty, together with any costs that may accrue in addition thereto) ***shall be a lien*** *in favor of the United States* ***upon all property and rights to property****, whether real or personal, belonging to such person.* [Emphasis added.}

To be valid, a federal tax lien has to be in writing and state the following information:

1. The IRS District where the tax was assessed.
2. An official document number or serial number.
3. A statement that demand for payment was made, but the liability remains unpaid.
4. Name and residence of taxpayer.
5. Taxpayer's identifying number (social security, etc.).
6. Kind of tax and tax period ending.
7. Date of each assessment (if more than one).
8. Unpaid balance of each assessment.
9. Grand total of all unpaid balances and costs.

10. Date, signature, and title of IRS official.

The IRS, as much as it would like to and tries, cannot "crowd out" other security interests that may have predated the IRS lien. Said prior interests (car loans, retail purchases, property taxes, mortgages, insurance contracts, mechanics liens, promissory note holders, etc.) are protected by Section 6323 and by other state and local laws. Section 6323 is titled: ***Validity and Priority Against Certain Persons***. It has 10 subsections, (a) through (j), comprising approximately 3,500 words. Its gist is that the IRS has to "get in line." However, an IRS lien becomes a priority attachment to all property acquired by the taxpayer subsequent to the recorded assessment date.

Often, legal questions arise concerning the validity and priority of federal tax liens. There are also special rules that apply to the filing of liens, releases of liens, discharges of property, and administrative appeals concerning erroneous liens. Going into detail on these matters is beyond the scope of our discussion. They are all covered in Section 6323. As a substitute, however, we present in Figure 9.2 some of the important features of IRS practices that may be instructive to you. An IRS lien can "stay on the books" for 10 years, and is *renewable each year* after that! [Sec. 6323(g).]

How a Levy Works

A lien is like a great big fishing net cast over all property and rights to property of a delinquent taxpayer. It prevents that property from being disposed of, without the knowledge and consent of the IRS. The lien, in and of itself, does not force the sale and conversion of the property. Any dispositional decision is left up to the taxpayer. The IRS has a prior claim to the sale proceeds before the taxpayer can claim them.

In contrast, a levy is a preemptive seizure of money and payables (mostly) that are due the taxpayer by third parties: payers, obligors, custodians, debtors, borrowers, bankers, etc. A levy is a command to a *selected payer* to turn over to the IRS *all* money, credits, bank deposits, and other obligations owed to the taxpayer. When this is done, the payer (addressee of the levy) must reply and report to the IRS. If the amount of the asset levied upon is insuffient to cover the amount of tax (plus penalties), additional assets may be levied upon.

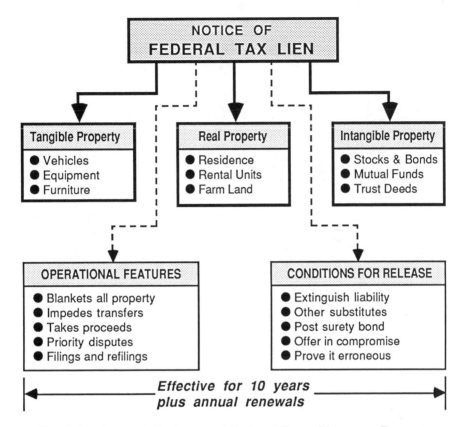

Fig. 9.2 - General Features of Federal Tax Liens on Property

A separate Notice of Levy is sent to each selected obligor to the taxpayer. The official instructions on the face of the notice say in very domineering terms that—

All property, rights to property, money, credits, and bank deposits now in your possession and belonging to this taxpayer (or for which you are obligated) and all money or other obligations you owe this taxpayer, are levied upon for payment of the tax, plus all additions provided by law. Demand is made on you to either pay this tax liability or pay any smaller amount that you owe this taxpayer. [Said amount(s)] **must be held for 21 calendar days** *from the day you receive this, before you send us the money.*

Serving notice of intent to levy, before actually executing the levy, allows the taxpayer 21 days to pay the levied amount himself or to make other arrangements. The general format and information in the taxpayer's *copy* of the levy is presented in Figure 9.3.

Form 668-A	**IRS NOTICE OF LEVY**

To: _____
(Name & address of payer being served)

IRS District _____
Phone Contact _____

Reply: _____
(By payer to IRS)

Name & Address of Taxpayer
_____
_____
_____

SSN: _____

Kind of Tax	Period(s) Ending	Unpaid Balance	Statutory Additions	Total
/////////////		**TOTAL AMOUNT DUE** ▶		

Interest and late payment penalty figured to ____ (date) _____

☐ This is your copy of a Notice of Levy we have sent to collect the amount you owe. We intend to send additional levies, if this one does not result in full payment . . . . . . The person this levy was sent to must turn over your property, money, credits, etc. to us just as though you had demanded it.

Signature of IRS Official /s/	**Title:**

Fig. 9.3 - Edited Version of Notice of Levy to Taxpayer

What happens if the obligor fails to turn the taxpayer's money over the IRS?

Answer: The obligor becomes personally liable to the IRS for the taxpayer's liability, and, in addition, is assessed a 50% enforcement penalty. This transfer of liability is made quite clear in the pertinent parts of Section 6332: *Surrender of Property Subject to Levy*. In particular, subsection (d): *Enforcement of Levy*, says that —

*(1) Any person who fails or refuses to surrender any property, or rights to property, subject to levy . . . **shall be liable in his own person and estate** to the* [IRS] *in a sum equal to the value of the property or rights not so surrendered,* [and] *. . . (2) In addition, . . . **shall be liable for a penalty equal to 50 percent** of the amount recoverable.* [Emphasis added.]

Obviously, no obligor of yours who receives a notice of levy is going to voluntarily assume your tax liability. As a "reward" for acting as a deputy tax collector, subsection 6332(e) [Effect of Honoring Levy] protects the obligor from any lawsuits that you might institute for recovering money that was turned over to the IRS on your behalf.

How Levy Can Cause Death

What we present to you here is NOT a hypothetical "scenario." It is an accurate account (abbreviated) of a real life — and death— story of a delinquent taxpayer. Ever so sadly, Taxpayer AFL (recall our Introduction) did not even realize that he was delinquent. He filed automatic extension forms for 1987 and 1988, and paid his accountant advance fees to prepare the corresponding returns. The accountant left town and retired to another state. No proper returns were ever filed.

AFL was a technologist with a Master's Degreee in Electrical Engineering. He was employed regularly for about 25 years, when he was laid off in August 1985 at the age of 50. After seeking re-employment for nearly two years, he started his own business in March 1987. He borrowed $17,000 from his friends and business associates. He rented an office and shop space, and obtained small R & D contracts. The R & D contracts expired in February 1989. Subsequently, he had to discontinue his business as he was unable to pay his bills. Several months later, his wife filed for divorce and for custody of his two children. He had to vacate his home and quit-claim it to his ex-wife.

Between early 1989 and late 1994, he was unemployed. He lived out of his car and with friends. He lived solely on unemployment compensation, on temporary work barterings, and on the proceeds from selling his meager assets, including his car and computer. He was some $30,000 in debt, including child-support arrearage.

About six months after becoming regularly employed, the employer (as described in our Introduction) handed AFL an IRS Levy Notice for $82,129 ($21,877 for 1987; $60,252 for 1988). Upon this, the employer turned over to the IRS the taxpayer's entire take-home pay check amounting to $2,312. This left AFL penniless. He couldn't buy food; he couldn't pay rent on his one-room apartment; he couldn't pay any of his other prior bills due. Needless to say, AFL was distraught and distressed.

The levy was served upon AFL on April 27, 1995. With the help of the author herein, he prepared and filed his 1987 and 1988 returns. Each return consisted of: (a) Form 1040, (b) Schedule C (Profit or loss from business), (c) Schedule SE (Self-employment tax), (d) Form 4562 (Depreciation allowance), and (e) Form 4571 (Explanation for late filing). His 1987 return showed no tax due — ABSOLUTELY NONE! It was filed on May 17, 1995 (some eight years late). His 1988 return showed no income tax due, but there was $253 in self-employment tax due. The 1988 was filed on May 18, 1995 (some seven years late).

On May 31, 1995, AFL died of massive cardiac hemorrhage. He died on his employer's premises where paramedics were called in. The official medical diagnosis was—

Massive Hernopericardium and Cardiac Tamponade

There is no doubt that the anxiety and stress brought on by the levy was the direct cause of AFL's death. His body was cremated on June 9, 1995. That was 43 days (April 17 to June 9) from life to ashes! This is THE ULTIMATE consequence of collection enforcement.

Refund Due Deceased Taxpayer

Collection enforcement does not stop upon the death of a taxpayer. The levy continues on into his estate. In AFL's case, the IRS had already seized $18,236 in wages and refunds. It was seeking another $63,893 (82,129 – 18,236) from his estate.

Accordingly, on September 2, 1995 (some 84 days after AFL's death), the IRS wrote to AFL's tax representative as follows:

Because your client is deceased, I must inquire about a possible estate and probate in order to resolve this case. Did your client leave an estate? Is there a probate? If so, please provide all the documents and information. . . . [Otherwise], I must investigate your client's assets for enforcement of the estate tax lien.

/s/_____
Revenue Officer

AFL's representative responded as follows:

It appears that the IRS has overseized about $17,520 from this destitute man. This is the only "asset" that he had. He had no home (it went to his ex-wife); he had no car (he couldn't make the payments); he had no bank account (he exhausted it all during his periods of unemployment); he had no credit card (no credit rating); and there are outstanding medical and funeral expenses which are yet to be paid. No California probate is required when a decedent's estate is less than $60,000 (CPC ¶ 13,100).

/s/_____
Tax Representative

At last, the IRS was boxed in its own corner. Other than AFL's personal clothing and effects, there were no assets for the IRS to seize. There was no estate: no probate. There was absolutely nothing left — except AFL's cremated body ashes — against which the IRS could enforce collection.

At this stage, final closure of the levy case seemed inevitable. During the next several months, the IRS returned the following overseized amounts, plus statutory interest, to AFL's executrix:

Date	Amount	Interest
11-17-95	4,866	547
12-15-95	12,654	1,419
	17,520	1,966

Total   19,486

Still, a "final/final" Form 1040 had to be filed for AFL's year of death (1995). Indeed, said return was filed on February 14, 1966. As it turned out, AFL was due a **refund** in the amount of $2,521 for his death year.

When a refund is due a deceased taxpayer, an entirely new form comes into play. Very few persons know of it; it's a tax-rights-after-death affair. Required is **Form 1310:** *Statement of Person Claiming Refund Due a Deceased Taxpayer.* The general arrangement of this form is presented in Figure 9.4.

FORM **1310**	REFUND DUE A DECEASED TAXPAYER	
Year decedent was due refund ▶ _____	Date of death ▶ _____	
Name of decedent _____	Decedent's SSN _____	
///// Name & address of claimant	_____	
I am filing this statement as:		
A ☐ Surviving spouse. **B** ☐ Court appointed representative. **C** ☐ Person other than **A** or **B**.	Check only one box	
Complete only if you checked Box **C**.		
	Yes	No
1. Did decedent leave a will?		
2. a. Has a personal representative been appointed? b. If "No", will one be appointed?		
3. If "No" to 2b, will you pay out the refund according to state law?	/////	
Signature and Verification	Signature of person claiming refund: /s/ _____	____ (date)

Fig. 9.4 - General Format/Contents of Form 1310

The significance of Form 1310 is that a claimant does not have to be a court appointed "personal representative" (meaning: an attorney) to close out federal tax matters for a decedent. Furthermore, the claimant can be any person named in the decedent's will as executor (or executrix). The claimant form is attached to the lower two-thirds of the front of Form 1040. At the top of Form 1040, the bold red words: FINAL RETURN: T/P DECEASED _____(date)_____ are hand printed.

How Seizure Works

If lien and levy do not produce enough money to pay the balance of tax due, the IRS institutes its ultimate enforcement weapon: SEIZURE AND SALE. It physically takes possession of designated property, removes it to a government compound (if practical), and prepares it for public auction. It sells it to the highest bidder at or over a *minimum price*. The minimum price is set at 50% of the lowest realistic market value that IRS appraisers estimate its worth to be.

The seizure of one or more property items takes place at unannounced times. This is to keep the taxpayer and his possessory friends off guard. Seizure is affected by affixing a sticker or attaching a tag to the designated property. The sticker or tag reads: **Property of the United States Government.** Following this bold caption are warnings about trespassing and penalties for interference with the enforcement of law. Two IRS agents are sent to carry out the seizure process.

Seizing private property by government agents is an infuriating experience. Some delinquent taxpayers become so enraged that they are willing to attack the IRS agents with clubs, chains, and even guns. Partly for their self protection and partly for enforcing their seizure actions, the designated agents are armed.

It is not until *after* the property is seized that the owner or possessor thereof is notified. For this purpose, Form 2433: *Notice of Seizure*, is used. The notice is signed by each of the two agents making the seizure.

The seizure and sale of a delinquent taxpayer's property is expressly authorized by Section 6331(b). Tangible personal property is the most likely target for seizures. This includes automobiles, trucks, tractors, trailers, campers, boats, airplanes, motorcycles, machinery, equipment, antiques, fine art, coin collections, and other movable objections. Items located in public places do not require a search warrant for seizure purposes. Items located on business premises or in personal residences do require a search warrant for entry purposes only. If the proceeds are insufficient to pay off the entire balance due, successive seizures are authorized [Sec. 6331(c)].

Items Exempt From Levy

Levy and seizure go hand in hand. Whereas levy is the seizure of monetary assets, seizure is the taking of physical assets. In theory, the IRS cannot levy and seize every last penny and every last item of property that a delinquent taxpayer has. He is supposed to be allowed sufficient assets to earn a living and pay for the necessities of life. This, in theory, is the rationale for Section 6334: *Property Exempt From Levy.* The net effect is that one is reduced to the official *poverty level* for living in the U.S.

Example items exempt from seizure are enumerated in Section 6334(a) as—

1. Wearing apparel and school books
2. Fuel, provisions, furniture, and personal effects (not exceeding $2,500 in value)
3. Tools of a trade, business, or profession (not exceeding $1,250 in value)
4. Unemployment benefits
5. Workmen's compensation
6. Judgments for the support of minor children
7. Principal residence (ordinarily)

In addition, a certain amount of wages and salary are exempt from levy, depending on one's filing status [Sec. 6334(d)]. For a single person, the exempt amount is approximately $130 per week ($6,750 per year); for a married couple: $230 per week ($12,000 per year); for parents with two children: $330 per week ($17,000 per year). All of these are approximate amounts; they are indexed for inflation each year.

As unbelievable as it may sound, the IRS can levy and seize upon one's social security benefits, pension and retirement plans (private, government, military), IRA plans, veteran's benefits, etc. Since these are steady long-term payouts, a special rule applies. It is Section 6331(h): *Continuing Levy on Certain Payments.* Up to 15 percent of one's retirement benefits can be seized . . . indefinitely. If one leaves an estate, even death does not discharge the enforcement power of collection activites.

10

WRONGFUL LEVIES & HARDSHIPS

Once In The Collection Enforcement "Grinder,"
Various Requests And Appeals Can Be Made
To Ease The Financial Pressures And
Emotional Stresses That Are Brought On.
Since 1954, The IRS Had Ample Authority To
Apply PRESSURE EASING Voluntarily. It Did
Nothing; It Kept The Pressure Up. In 1988 And
Again In 1996, New Tax Laws MANDATED The
IRS to Treat Its "Customers" More Decently.
Now There Are Procedures For Relief From
Hardship, Installment Payments, Withdrawal of
Liens, Release Of Levies, Return Of Seized
Property, And, As A "Last Resort," Offer In
Compromise.

Prior to 1988 (Taxpayer Rights Act 1), the IRS was rather callous about its liens, levies, and seizures. It was a "macho thing" to destroy a few taxpayers in order to instill fear in the vast taxpaying public. The IRS's macho business led to many wrongful levies, erroneous seizures, and dire economic hardships. Many tales of the IRS's villainy surfaced before Congress, which finally got the word. As a result, today the agency is a little more careful before throwing its weight around. The Rights Act 2 (1996) has helped to prod improvements along.

Still, further improvements in IRS behavior are needed. Unbridled enforcement power has a drugging effect on entrenched managers and employees. The effect doesn't wear off easily. Particularly so today, where electronic Big Brothering and Surveillance are so advanced and instantaneous. Financial and emotional hardships can be showered on a delinquent taxpayer with the slightest touch of a computer key or click of a mouse.

Once you have been notified by the IRS that you are a delinquent taxpayer (in its eyes), there ARE THINGS that you can do to ease the enforcement pressures to which you are subjected. The problem is, the easing procedures are not clear cut, nor are they simple. You must apply persevering effort to convince a skeptical collection agent that your circumstances are what you say they are. Yes, there are collection appeal rights, installment payment arrangements, and procedures for releasing a lien, releasing a levy, and restoring seized property. But none of these easing procedures can be commenced until you've filed all proper returns and have made full disclosure of your financial affairs.

Explaining these matters is what this chapter is all about.

Example: Erroneous Levy

Although behavioral improvements by the IRS are underway, there still arise situations where the IRS exercises its enforcement powers erroneously. A recent case in point is that of a merchant mariner who never owed any tax, but whose bank accounts were levied and seized surreptitiously and repeatedly three years in a row. Let us explain.

The taxpayer, DRM, a single man (U.S. citizen), lived and worked abroad on an oil drilling ship for three years. He worked for a Texas oil exploration company in the Norwegian Sea, Persian Gulf, China Sea, and Philippine Sea. He was on foreign duty more than 330 days each year. This qualified him for the $70,000 per annum foreign earned income **exclusion** of **Section 911**: *Citizens Living Abroad*. Because DRM earned less than the $70,000 exclusion amount per year, his Texas employer withheld no income tax whatsoever. This was proper, as no U.S. income tax is due from eligible citizens working overseas.

For the years at issue, DRM's earnings averaged about $55,000 per year. Of this amount, he sent about $35,000 each year to a bank in California where his mother lived. Actually, he owed no income tax: NONE! Nevertheless, the IRS levied upon his bank accounts and took all of his savings — nearly $93,000.

There is no question that it was a wrongful levy. But how does one stop a wrongful levy or seizure by the IRS?

Answer: For most situations, you can't. Once enforcement is executed, you have to see it through. Then — and only then — can you approach the IRS to correct its wrongdoing.

In the merchant mariner case above, the taxpayer had to file tax returns for each of the three years that were levied upon. To each return, he had to complete and attach **Form 2555**: *Foreign Earned Income*. He readily qualified for the $70,000 annual exclusion. Many months later, the IRS returned his entire $93,000 plus a little interest. There were no apologies from the IRS.

In another case (foreign traveling), while no wrongful levy was executed, a wrongful IRS demand for payment was made.

A single taxpayer, secretary, worked for two employers during the year. The employers withheld a total of $7,327 federal income tax from her pay. She went on a long vacation to South America where she contracted a debilitating sickness. When she returned from vacation she was so weakened that she forgot all about filing her short-form return 1040EZ. About five years later, the IRS sent her a statutory return for the missing year, showing $10,025 as due and payable ($7,555 tax plus $2,470 penalties). The IRS gave her no credit whatsoever for her $7,327 in withholdings. She filed her return and properly claimed the withholdings (with the W-2s attached). She attached a check for $228 (the additional tax due) with a statement explaining the cause of her failure to file to file on time.

About 60 days later, the IRS's response was:

We have applied the payment of $228 to the account identified above. Your account is paid in full as of this time.

These two cases illustrate the key point of this chapter. When notified by the IRS of what it perceives to be a delinquency on your part, you must respond. Don't grumble about the IRS picking on you or engaging in a personal vendetta against you. Do that which is constructive and positive. If you haven't filed a tax return when you should have, get busy and file it! In Figure 10.1 we present an overview of the various positive steps to take.

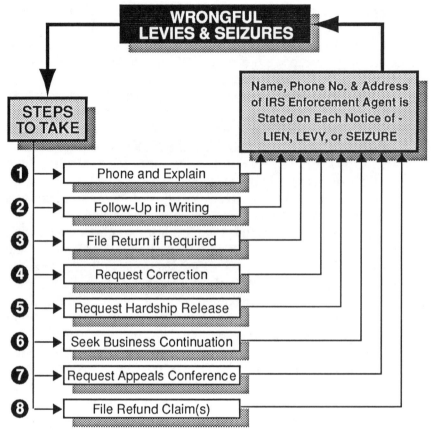

Fig. 10.1 - What To Do Generally if Wrongful Collection By IRS

Seek Release of Levy

If matters get beyond an erroneous billing, and money and property have been seized from you, you need to be aware of Tax Code **Section 6343**. This section is titled: *Authority to Release Levy and Return Property.* The gist of its subsection (a) is that the IRS must release the levy promptly if—

1. The liability for such levy is satisfied,
2. The release will facilitate collection of the correct liability,
3. The taxpayer has agreed to make installment payments on the liability,

4. The levy is creating **an economic hardship** on the taxpayer due to his financial condition, or
5. The levy is upon essential property which prevents a taxpayer from carrying on his trade or business.

The fact that it has been legislatively necessary to make corrective provisions in the enforcement laws attests to the many — sometimes despicable — wrongdoings of the IRS. Nevertheless, you are the one who has to initiate the positive steps for correcting the IRS.

Subsection 6343(b) goes on to say that—

If . . . property has been wrongfully levied upon, it shall be lawful for the [IRS] *to return—*
(1)   the specific property levied upon,
(2)   an amount of money equal to the amount of money levied upon, or
(3)   an amount of money equal to the amount of money received . . . from a sale of such property.
Property may be returned at any time. . . . Interest shall be allowed and paid at the [regular] *overpayment rate.*

If you have received a coy of Notice of Levy, contact the IRS person or phone number designated, and inquire what you need to do to get the levy released. Explain that it is causing undue hardship and hampers your earning a living.

"Significant Hardship" Defined

In 1988, the first time ever, Congress enacted **Section 7811**: *Taxpayer Assistance Orders*. This one Code section alone breathed new life and new hope into tax justice for all. This hope flickered until 1996 when Congress added more teeth to Section 7811. It designated a "Taxpayer Advocate" within the IRS.

Of particular interest to us at this moment is subsection (a) of Section 7811. This subsection: *Authority to Issue*, reads in principal part as—

*Upon application filed by a taxpayer with the Office of the Taxpayer Advocate . . ., the Taxpayer Advocate may issue a **Taxpayer Assistance Order** if, in the determination of the Taxpayer Advocate, the taxpayer is **suffering or is about to suffer a significant hardship** as a result of the manner in which the internal revenue laws are being administered.* [Emphasis added.]

Particularly note the last phrase above: *as a result of the manner in which . . .* the tax laws are being administered. This is clear statutory admission that the IRS abuses its authority.

Also note the emphasized phrase: [the taxpayer] *is suffering or about to suffer a significant hardship.* This raises the question: What is meant by a "significant hardship"?

The term is not defined in IRC Section 7811 itself. It is defined in rather general terms in Regulation 301.7811-1(a)(4)(ii) as—

*The term "significant hardship" means a **serious privation** caused or about to be caused to the taxpayer as the result of the particular manner in which the internal revenue laws are being administered by the Internal Revenue Service. Mere economic or personal inconvenience to the taxpayer does not constitute significant hardship. Instead, even where financial hardship is involved, a finding of "significant hardship" will depend on an examination of the action taken, or to be take by the Internal Revenue Service which produces or would produce the financial hardship. The action or proposed action must be such that it would **offend the sense of fairness of taxpayers** in general were they aware of all the surrounding facts and circumstances.* [Emphasis added.]

What "offends the sense of fairness of taxpayers" is a matter of judgment. Certainly, the levy and seizure of property which puts a noncriminal taxpayer out of business, or forces him into unemployment, would be a significant hardship. Certainly, too, would be the levying of all bank accounts, escrow accounts, and investment accounts of any individual, thereby preempting his mortgage payments and forcing his home into foreclosure. Or, preempting money intended for medical insurance and hospital payments for major surgery or disabling illness. Would it not also constitute significant hardship — emotionally speaking — to insist on an audit examination of a female taxpayer who had just been criminally raped, or of a male taxpayer just recovering from multiple bypass heart surgery? Does a taxpayer always have to be driven into a state of depression, despair, or near-suicide?

TAO Application: Form 911

Section 7811: Taxpayer Assistance Orders, went into effect on January 1, 1989. To enable a taxpayer, or his representative, or an IRS employee to make application for a TAO, a new tax form had to be devised. Said application is now designated as **Form 911**.

It is not clear how the number 9-1-1 evolved, but we think it has to do with the emergency telephone number 911 used commonly throughout the United States. It is a number that most taxpayers can identify with when they need emergency-type assistance. An IRS form using this same number makes sense.

The official title of Form 911 is: APPLICATION FOR TAXPAYER ASSISTANCE ORDER . . . **For Relief from Hardship**. Instructions on the back of the form tell you—

Do not use this application to contest the amount of any tax you owe. If you disagree with the amount of tax assessed, see Publication 1, Your Rights as a Taxpayer.

The instructions also say—

Please tell us what kind of relief you are requesting. We will contact you after our review to advise you of our decision.

If you have a correctly assessed tax liability, and a levy on all of your wages and accounts, but can make other arrangements for payment, by all means request other payment arrangements. If you have suffered emotional or physical trauma recently, and your returns have been selected for audit, request a postponement until you are medically cleared. In all situations where relief is granted, the statute of limitations for determining or collecting tax is suspended [Sec. 7811(d)].

Pursuant to Section 7811(b), if your Form 911 is approved, the Taxpayer Advocate may require the responsible IRS function—

(1)   to release property of the taxpayer levied upon, or

(2)   to cease any action, or refrain from taking any action with respect to—

   (A)   the collection of tax,

   (B)   bankruptcy and receivership,

   (C)   discovery of liability and enforcement, or

   (D)   any other provision of law which is specifically described by the Taxpayer Advocate in such order.

Contrary to some misconceptions, Form 911 assistance cannot forgive any tax, penalty, or interest. All it can do is ease the pressure of collection enforcement. It is simply a means of buying time and the chance to regain one's composure.

Installment Payments

It is not the function of the IRS to collect tax by destroying a taxpayer's livelihood. On the other hand, if one owes tax, knows that he owes tax, and does not dispute its correctness, one is expected to pay that tax. If one is unable to pay currently, arrangements for monthly installments can be made. This is the substance of Section 6159: *Agreements for Payment of Tax Liability in Installments*. Section 6159 is another of those Taxpayer Rights initiatives enacted by Congress in 1988 (and strengthened in 1996).

The policy guideline is set forth in subsection 6159(a): *Authorization of Agreements*. It reads in full as—

The [IRS] is authorized to enter into written agreements with any taxpayer under which such taxpayer is allowed to satisfy liability for payment of any tax in installment payments if the [IRS] determines that such agreement will facilitate collection of such liability.

In order for the IRS to determine if installments will facilitate the collection of tax, one has to request an installment arrangement. The form for this purpose is **Form 9465**: *Installment Agreement Request.* This is a single page form with a headnote that reads—

Caution: A Notice of Federal Tax Lien may be filed to protect the government's interest until you pay in full.

The form also warns you that a user fee will be charged, and that all *penalties and interest* will continue until full payment is made.

Approval of an installment request is not an absolute right of a taxpayer. Approval is contingent upon the IRS's judgment call that the tax eventually will be paid. Collection is in jeopardy when a taxpayer actively engages in the dissipation and concealment of assets to place them beyond the reach of the IRS.

In the majority of cases, approval is granted where the taxpayer indicates a willingness and capability to pay the remaining balance due within one year of the original due date. If payment over a period of more than one year is requested, the requester has to file an exhaustive financial disclosure statement.

Financial Disclosure Statements

As you should suspect, the IRS has its own financial disclosure forms that it wants you to complete. There are two such forms:

Form 433-A: *Collection Information Statement for Individuals*
Form 433-B: *Collection Information Statement for Businesses*

Each is a full 4-page form with approximately 100 entry lines, blocks, and checkboxes to complete. In no way are we going to present all details of each form. We just want you to be aware of their existence and their general contents as outlined in Figure 10.2.

The IRS classifies your financial disclosures as *Collection Information* statements. The idea behind this classification is that the IRS wants to know where your money pockets and property

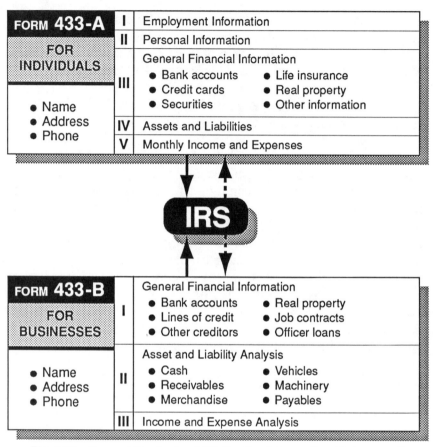

Fig. 10.2 - General Contents of "Collection Information Statements"

assets are. It needs this information for its liens, levies, and seizures ... should collection enforcement become necessary. The IRS has no intention of treating your installment request as a loan of money or approval of your credit. Basically, it wants all tax due NOW, but may allow installments if it can levy or seize your assets should you default on any part of the payment agreement.

A headnote instruction on each "collection information" form (in Figure 10.2) reads—

*NOTE: **Complete all blocks, except shaded areas. Write "N/A"** (not applicable) in those blocks that do not apply.*

This instruction forces you to read every entry line, every block, and every checkbox, and either answer accurately or write in "N/A", as applicable. Any omissions are deemed to be a willful attempt to misstate or cover up your collection-target assets.

A highly generalized listing of items that the IRS targets for collection enforcement includes:

1. Cash on hand
2. Bank account balances
3. Investment account holdings
4. Money owed to you by others
5. Loan value of your life insurance
6. Credit balances on credit cards
7. Wages, salaries, bonuses, and tips
8. Interest, dividends, and rental income
9. Equity in your home or other realty
10. Equity in any business you may own

After listing all of your assets and liabilities, you are required to summarize your version of income and expenses (on a monthly basis for individuals, or on an annual or other periodic basis for businesses). Your version of your expenses involved are examined closely by the IRS, and compared with *minimum* national norms.

Requesting Withdrawal of Lien

If there is the slightest doubt about the ultimate collection of tax, the IRS will file automatically a Notice of Federal Tax Lien. Formerly, paper forms (Form 668-F) were used. Today, the filings are done electronically. Electronic liens are transmitted to the County Recorder's Office where the taxpayer resides and where his property is physically located. Rarely does a taxpayer ever know that a tax lien has been filed. The IRS is not required to notify a taxpayer of such action. One usually learns of a lien from a creditor, or from his bank or other account holder.

A federal tax lien can ruin a person's credit rating and his access to credit with financial institutions and business suppliers. It can also affect his relationship with his employer. These and other misapplication potentials were recognized in the Rights Act 2. It added subsection 6323(j) to the IR Code effective July 30, 1996.

Subsection 6323(j) is titled: *Withdrawal of Notice in Certain Circumstances.* Its essence is—

> *The* [IRS] *may withdraw a notice of a lien filed . . . if* [it] *determines that—*
>
> *(A) the filing . . . was premature or not in accordance with procedures,*
>
> *(B) the taxpayer has entered into an agreement . . . to satisfy the tax liability for which the lien was imposed,*
>
> *(C) the withdrawal . . . will facilitate the collection of the tax liability, or*
>
> *(D) the withdrawal . . . would be in the best interest of the taxpayer (as determined by the Taxpayer Advocate) and the United States.*
>
> *Any such withdrawal shall be made by filing notice at the same office as the withdrawn notice.* *A copy of such notice of withdrawal shall be provided to the taxpayer.* [Emphasis added.]

The IRS will not withdraw a lien voluntarily on its own. You must specifically request the withdrawal. Currently, there is no official form for doing so. When you first learn of the lien, make the request initially by phone, then follow up in writing. A suggested format for your request is presented in Figure 10.3.

Indicate that you are making the request pursuant to IRC Section 6323(j). Stress which of the subparagraphs (A), (B), (C), or (D) is/are most applicable. Give a plausible basis for your belief. Follow with the subsequent request that, if withdrawal is made, the IRS notify your creditors, financial institutions, and others whom you designate. Upon your specific request, the IRS is **required** to notify credit agencies and other credit-interest entities. Subsection 6323(j)(2): *Notice to Credit Agencies, Etc.* says that—

> *The* [IRS] *shall promptly make reasonable efforts to notify* [whom you designate] *of the withdrawal of* [the notice of lien].

Your Address	Reference Date
	• IRS Document No.
To IRS office of last contact	• Form or Notice No.
	• Tax Year(s)
	• Your Name & Tax ID

REQUEST WITHDRAWAL OF LIEN
& NOTIFICATION OF CREDITORS

1. As per IRC Sec. 6323 (j)(1), it is requested that the Federal Tax Lien filed against me be withdrawn. The grounds on which this request is made are:

(A) ☐ The filing was premature, erroneous, or not in accordance with procedures _____ (attach backup) _____

(B) ☐ Have entered into an installment agreement to satisfy the tax liability _____ (cite date) _____

(C) ☐ Withdrawal will facilitate collection of tax
(explain how)
_____

(D) ☐ Withdrawal is recommended by the Taxpayer Advocate
(attach relevant document)
_____

2. As per IRC Sec. 6323 (j)(2), if this request is granted, it is further requested that the following creditors be notified:

(a) _____
(b) _____
(c) _____

yours truly,

_____ (dated) _____   /s/ _____

Fig. 10.3 - Format for Requesting Withdrawal of Federal Tax Lien

Too often in the past, the IRS has irreparably damaged a taxpayer's credit standing and business reputation, and walked away scot-free. Section 6323(j) is intended to be protection against continuing this practice . . . ad infinitum.

Appealing Levies & Seizures

In 1988 (Rights Act 1), Congress added still another new section to the IR Code. This was Section 6326: *Administrative Appeal of Liens.* Although designated for appealing liens, the procedures apply similarly to levies, seizures, and termination of installment agreements. As to matters of levies, seizures, and terminations, the taxpayer is notified in advance, in writing. This prenotification is not required for liens. Hence, Congress felt it necessary to address this "silent area" of tax law. Other related tax laws address (1) *Release of Lien* [Sec. 6325(a)], (2) *Discharge of Property* [Sec. 6325(b)], (3) *Subordination of Lien* [Sec. 6325(d)], (4) *Nonattachment of Lien* [Sec. 6325(e)], (5) *Release of Levy* [Sec. 6343(a)], and (6) *Return of Property* [Sec. 6343(b)].

Section 6326 starts off by saying—

In such form and at such time as the [IRS] shall prescribe by regulations, any person shall be allowed to appeal . . .

The emphasized phrase "in such form" required the IRS to come up with a special collection appeal form. After some 10 years of bureaucratic procrastination, there is now **Form 9423**: *Collection Appeal Request.* In addition to identifying the requesting taxpayer and the tax matters involved, the main body of the form consists of two main parts, namely:

I — *Collection Action Appealed*

☐ *Federal Tax Lien*
☐ *Levy or Notice of Levy*
☐ *Seizure*
☐ *Termination of Installment Agreement*

II — *Explanation*

Why you disagree with the collection action(s) you checked above and how you would resolve your tax problem. Attach copies of any documents that you think will support your position.

The instructions to Form 9423 go on to say—

If an appeal is requested after a seizure is made, the appeal must be requested with the Collection Manager within 10 business days after the Notice of Seizure is provided to you or left at your home or business.

Normally, we will stop the collection action you disagree with until your appeal is settled. [However], *false information, omitting pertinent information, or fraud will void any appeal decision . . . and collection action will resume.*

Your basis for any collection appeal is the same as depicted in Figure 10.3, namely: alleging of error, wrongfulness, impropriety, improvidence, hardship, etc. Your appeal must be bona fide, and not frivolous or for purposes of delay.

"Last Resort": OIC

Suppose that you have tried all of the above disagreeing actions, and that none of them have sufficiently relieved the collection enforcement pressures on you. And further, suppose that there is no possible way to ever pay off the tax liability that you agree is correct. Your financial fortunes have worsened to the point where you and your family cannot sleep at night. The worry, distress, and despair are getting to you. Is there one last resort you can try?

Yes, there is. It is called: *Offer in Compromise* (OIC).

The OIC concept was first enacted in 1954. It was designated as Section 7122: *Compromises*. At that time, all OICs over $500 in tax liability had to be submitted to the General Counsel of the Treasury Department who in turn had to confer with the Attorney General of the Justice Department. Consequently, for the past 40 years, very few OICs were ever accepted by the IRS. In 1996

(Rights Act 2), Congress softened the tortuous formality of OICs by raising the rigidity threshold from $500 to $50,000. As a result, the 1996 amendment opened the door to more reasonable eligibility standards for distressed taxpayers.

Section 7122 itself does not explain the process involved, nor does it indicate what the primary grounds are for acceptance of an offer in compromise. Such details must be sought elsewhere. This is where Regulation 301.7122-1 comes into play. Said regulation consists of about 1,000 words. These words are organized into eight subregulations: (a) through (g). A synopsis overview of these subregulations is presented in Figure 10.4. This figure is important as a guideline of what to do and expect, should you be an eligible candidate for compromise consideration.

IRC Section 7122: COMPROMISES

REG. 301.7122-1: Offers in Compromise

Subreg.	Heading	Contents
(a)	In General	Grounds for doubt as to collectibility
(b)	Scope of Agreement	Any liability for tax, penalty, or interest
(c)	Effect of Agreement	Conclusively settles all questions of liability
(d)	Procedure re Offers	Submission on IRS form, with remittance or deposit
(e)	Record (If Accepted)	By Chief Counsel of amount assessed, and actually paid
(f)	Re Statute of Limitations	Waived while offer pending, and for 1 year thereafter
(g)	Public Inspection	Confidential, except as authorized by Sec. 6103

Fig. 10.4 - Synopsis of Scope and Contents of Regulation 301.7122-1

The gist of Figure 10.4 is that, except where there has been a deliberate attempt to defraud or evade the tax system, a compromise agreement settles **all** tax issues. However, the settlement applies *only* to the specifically compromised year (or years), and does not affect other years where a tax liability is unpaid or may be unpaid. Furthermore, a settlement offer requires that you *waive* the statute of limitations against the IRS (for assessment or collection) for the period during which the offer is pending, and for one year thereafter.

Subregulation 301.7122-1(a) starts off by saying that—

Any [tax] *liability may be compromised upon one or both of the following two grounds:*

(1) Doubt as to liability; or

(2) Doubt as to collectibility.

No such liability will be compromised if the liability has been established by a valid judgment or is certain, and there is no doubt as to the ability of the Government to collect the amounts owing. [Emphasis added.]

Use OIC Form 656

In other words, as a last/last resort, there must exist a bona fide doubt as to the ultimate collectibility of the tax. If true doubt does indeed exist, the IRS views an OIC as a legitimate alternative to declaring a case uncollectible or to participating in protracted installment agreements of five years or more.

To prepare an offer, one must obtain **Form 656**: *Offer in Compromise*, and complete it diligently and faithfully. It is a 2-page form with page 1 consisting of entry spaces and checkboxes. Its page 2 consists of 15 conditions that one must agree to and sign (under penalties of perjury). Accompanying the form are six pages of instructions which focus primarily on **Form 433-A** (for individuals) and **Form 433-B** (for businesses). These are the two collection information statement forms that we generalized back in Figure 10.2. The instructions also provide worksheets and informational tips on how to make an adequate offer.

An offer is adequate if it reasonably reflects collection potential and is made up of the following components:

(1) the amount collectible from one's *existing assets*;
(2) the amount collectible from one's *present and future income*;
(3) the amount collectible from *third party transferees* (persons and entities who owe money or property to the offerer); and
(4) the amount collectible from one's *assets beyond the reach* of the IRS (in trusts, life estates, foreign jurisdictions, and disguised ownership arrangements).

The IRS does not consider an offer adequate for reasons other than on its legal ability to collect from the taxpayer. If an amount of tax is truly uncollectible, all of the huffing and puffing enforcement actions by the IRS are for naught.

To illustrate how the OIC process works, we flash back to the true case of taxpayer HEB in Chapter 2. When he can find work, he gross earns about $2,600 per month ($31,200 per year). After withholdings for a single person, his monthly take-home pay is about $1,800 (2,600 – 800). In November 1995, HEB received a Notice of Levy on his wages totaling $134,900 (for tax year 1988). Simultaneously, the IRS garnished $500 per month from his wages and applied it to the levy. HEB appealed on the basis of hardship. The garnishment was reduced to $250 pr month (or about $3,000 per year).

Simple arithmetic tells you that at the installment rate of $3,000 per year, it would take **45 years** before HEB could pay off his $134,900 levy (assuming no further penalties and interest). At the time of the levy, HEB was 56 years old. He had less than 10 years of work left, if he could find work for all years.

Even the IRS could see the handwriting on the wall. It would never be able to collect the $134,900 levy plus its continuing penalties and interest. Once the IRS became convinced of this, it was quite cooperative in processing HEB's offer. Finally, HEB's offer of $30,000 was accepted in March 1997. Thus, as far as the IRS was concerned, the 1988 tax liability was paid in full.

11

LITIGATION MATTERS

When Forced Into Litigation With The IRS, You — The Taxpayer — Have The Full Burden Of Proof. You Have To Designate A Tax Law On Which You Rely, Then You Have To Overcome The Barrage Of Alternative "Theories" The IRS Will Use Against You. For REDETERMINATION Of Tax Deficiencies And Penalties, The U.S. Tax Court Is Your Best Hope, Though It Does Exude A "Brother Agency" Syndrome Towards The IRS. Technically, If You Prevail, You MAY BE Awarded Attorney Fees [Sec. 7430]. Other Courts Where Tax Related Matters Can Be Heard Are The U.S. Claims Court (In Washington, D.C.) And Any U.S. District Court In A "Federal Building" Nearest You.

There is one deep-rooted, intransigent problem with the IRS. It has entirely too much power, and there are too few checks and balances against abuses of that power. The result is confrontation over tax matters, tax laws, and the behavior of tax agents.

Power breeds arrogance. This arrogance pervades the IRS bureaucracy at all levels. With its approximately 5,000 (mostly young) attorneys on the public payroll, this arrogance converts into a lot of litigious issues . . . just for the sport of it.

The IRS can — and does — force a disputive issue into court, because it knows that private attorney fees can themselves dissuade a taxpayer from continuing his case. With its virtually unlimited resources, the IRS can spend many thousands of dollars of public money just to prevent a taxpayer from winning a point. This is not justice; this is power. Short of outright conceding to the IRS, litigation may be the only way to resolve a tax dispute. But don't expect too much from the legal process.

In this chapter, we want to apprise you of the realities of litigation and of the various forums (courts) available to you. We want to tell you how to focus your case for best results, and to warn you against unethical practices of the IRS. When Big Government is your adversary, you are in a different litigious world. Adversarial extremes apply whether you seek redress in the U.S. Tax Court, U.S. Claims Court, or U.S. District Court. Once an IRS dispute exists, only federal courts will hear the matter.

A Leadoff Example

For tax disputes over $10,000, the first logical recourse is the U.S. Tax Court. Whether small or large cases, the procedures are much the same as we discussed in Chapter 8: Small Tax Court. The differences are greater formality, excessive pretrial discovery, IRS shenanigans, and endless haggling over trivia. The IRS clouds — and reclouds — any issue that is straightforward. For these and other reasons, a petitioner must engage a tax attorney and pay his/her $150 to $350 hourly fee. At *minimum*, one should figure an attorney's Tax Court attention time at from 50 to 100 hours. If the tax inequity is really important, attorney fees could easily run $50,000 or more.

Here's a good example of what a large Tax Court petition involves. Taxpayer GMM (true initials) received a Notice of Deficiency for $155,178 for tax year 1987. She received the notice in 1991. She and her ex-husband (a high-powered attorney) were divorced in 1989. The 1987 return was prepared and signed by a prestigious accounting firm at the request of the husband. GMM had no idea what was on the return. The husband never explained it to her, nor would he allow her to even glance at it. Yet, her signature (facsimiled) was thereon. The husband had long since moved from the marital residence to places unknown. So, the IRS went after the wife. She was truly an *innocent spouse*. She had no separate income; either she had to file a petition in Tax Court for relief, or pay the $155,178 plus interest.

A special tax code section authorizes the IRS to grant relief to an innocent spouse and go after the culprit spouse separately. On point is Section 6013(e): *Spouse Relieved of Liability in Certain Cases*. Following this law and its regulation to the letter, a 10-page petition was filed. It cited **eight specific errors** the IRS made in its assessment of GMM. In abbreviated form, these errors are presented in Figure 11.1. Note that the errors are grouped into a "Paragraph 4."

PETITION TO U.S. TAX COURT

Petitioner: _____ ; Respondent: Commissioner, IRS

Paragraph 4.	The determination of the tax set forth in said notice of deficiency (or liability) is based upon the following errors:

(a) It is an error to disregard the legislative intent of IRC Sec.6013(e) regarding innocent spouse relief.

(b) It is an error to disregard that the alleged deficiency is attributable principally to one spouse, namely: _____ (soc.sec.no.)

(c) It is an error to disregard that there is a substantial understatement of tax for which the petitioner is eligible for relief, pursuant to IRC Sec.6013(e)(4).

(d) It is an error to disregard that the attributable spouse in (b) above has entered grossly erroneous items on his/her portion of the tax return for _____ .

(e) It is an error to disregard that the grossly erroneous items in (d) above have no basis in fact or law.

(f) It is an error to disregard that petitioner, when signing the tax return at issue, did not know and had no reason for knowing, that there were grossly erroneous items thereon.

(g) It is an error to disregard the inequitableness of holding the petitioner liable for the grossly erroneous items above.

(h) It is an error not to relieve the petitioner from liability for tax and other amounts that derive from the grossly erroneous items.

... other matters in the petition

Fig. 11.1 - Assignments of Error for Innocent Spouse Petition

As required by procedure, for each alleged IRS error, there must be a corresponding statement of fact that points to why the IRS is wrong. All such facts are grouped into a "Paraagraph 5." For example, the lead-off fact in GMM's case read—

> *(a) Petitioner is a housewife who participated in no manner whatsoever in the preparation of the joint return 1987. Petitioner did not personally sign the return, but recalls vaguely signing a power of attorney designating the accounting firm of _____ to act as petitioner's agent.*

And similarly for paragraph 5(b) through (5(h).

> *WHEREFORE, petitioner prays that she be relieved of all liability for the $155,178 deficiency in tax for 1987.*

> */s/* _____

How the IRS "Responded"

When a petition is filed in Tax Court, the IRS has 60 days in which to answer. The IRS's answer is never objective. It is a denial of everything alleged by the taxpayer except his/her name, social security number, and the amount of tax in dispute. There is nothing meaningful in an IRS answer whatsoever. It is a perfunctory "joinder of the issue(s)" to commence a court fight.

Here's how the IRS responded to GMM's petition above:

> *THE RESPONDENT, in answer to the petition filed in the above-entitled case, admits, denies and alleges as follows:*
> *1. through 3., inclusive. Admits* [This is the petitioner's name, address, social security number, copy of deficiency notice, and amount of tax in dispute, namely: $155,178.]
> *4. (a) through (h), inclusive. Denies the allegations of error.*
> *5. (a) through (c), inclusive. Denies for lack of present knowledge.*
> *5. (d). Admits that the substantial understatement of tax resulted from the disallowance of $554,205 in capital loses, but denies for lack of present knowledge the remainder of the allegations.*
> *5. (e) through (h), inclusive. Denies for lack of present knowledge.*
> *6. Denies generally each and every allegation of the petition not hereinbefore specifically admitted, qualified or denied.*

WHEREFORE, it is prayed that the respondent's determination as set forth in the notice of deficiency, be in all respects approved.

Date _____   *Chief Counsel, IRS*
                            /s/ Assistant District Counsel

Obviously, the IRS is being hard-nosed . . . just for the thrill of it. It knows that the taxpayer will have to pay roughly $50,000 in attorney fees to fight the IRS in Tax Court. The IRS also knows that these fees will put additional pressure, pain, and suffering on the taxpayer. The IRS can't take any heat itself, but it loves to heap it onto a taxpayer.

In the situation above, do you concede and pay $155,178 in tax (plus penalty and interest) to avoid litigation? Or, do you pay some $50,000 in attorney fees to fight the IRS?

Once the IRS "answers" a petition, there is a follow-on process called *joinder and discovery*. Before any court hearing takes place, the IRS tries to beat down a petitioner and force concessions. When in its forcing mode, the IRS becomes nasty and unrelenting. This is one of those mysterious quirks of IRS behavior. It will try to defeat any Act of Congress that a taxpayer relies on to show how the IRS erred. Nevertheless, one must be persistent.

Editorial Postscript: During the joinder and discovery phase of the above TC petition, it became increasingly obvious to the IRS that it had no real case. The petitioner met "every letter" of the statutory relief provisions. Before actual trial, the IRS conceded the case totally and withdrew its deficiency notice.

Alternative Theory Barrage

As a taxpayer in litigation, you have to find a tax law that fits your case and rely on it. Except for fraud and tax evasion matters, the burden of proof is always on you. You have to prove that you come within the particular law on which you rely. You have to cite the law verbatim, cite the pertinent regulations thereunder, and cite any relevant prior court cases that support your position. And you must present clear-cut material facts and circumstances.

What does your adversary, the IRS, have to do?

All it has to do is put up a barrage of alternative legal theories — all totally academic — that some other disallowance law might conceivably, remotely, and potentially apply. This is where all the young IRS attorneys have a field day. They can educate themselves on various tax matter at your expense and agony.

To illustrate what we are getting at, consider Section 174: Research and Experimental Expenditures. This section comprises about 650 legal words. But you can get the gist of the Congressional intent in subsection 174(a)(1). This subsection: *Treatment as Expenses*, reads as follows:

> *A taxpayer may treat research or experimental expenditures which are paid or incurred by him during the taxable year in connection with his trade or business as expenses which are not chargeable to capital account. The expenditures so treated shall be allowed as a deduction.*

Anyone with common sense can read Section 174 and apply it. For example, a house painter could develop a portable scaffold and write off the expense. A tax accountant could develop a computer check-off program for testing office-in-home deductions. A dentist could fund a dental lab technician for developing a prophylactic gum device. The "bottom line" of Section 174(a) says: the expenditures **shall be allowed** as a deduction.

Yet, what happens when a small business owner tries to use Section 174? The IRS jumps all over him. It beats him down by disallowing the deduction and alleging that other theories apply. It is now a regular routine that the IRS goes through to defeat this particular tax law. It has been on the books since 1954, and has been changed very little since that time.

The IRS's defeat-the-law routine starts off by alleging that Section 183 — not 174 — applies. Section 183 is titled: *Activities Not Engaged in For Profit*. Any time you try to develop a new product or service, you, initially, never make a profit. So, according to the IRS, no deduction for your expenditures is allowed.

If the IRS can't get away with its Section 183 argument, it will next assert that Section 195 applies. Section 195 is titled: *Start-Up Expenditures*. This section says that no deduction is allowed unless the new product or service becomes successful, and then it is only allowed over a 60-month period.

If the IRS can't get away with its Section 195 assertion, it will argue that Section 263: *Capital Expenditures*, applies. Section

263 means that you get no deduction until you sell or abandon the item, product, or service that you have developed.

If the IRS can't get away with its Section 263 assertion, it will argue that Section 280A must apply. Section 280A is titled: *Disallowance of Certain Expenses in Connection With Business Use of Home.* Most small business owners use the premises of their home and garage for developing new products and services. This cuts down on overhead and other costs. In the IRS mind, such activities constitute a hobby and, therefore, no deduction is allowed.

On and on the IRS goes, trying to defeat a law (Section 174) which Congress enacted as an economic incentive for small businesses. Tax Court judges, particularly, love the IRS's alternative theory academia. It takes them back to their law school days when they practiced mock trials in the classroom. It seems that much of the IRS's litigious strategy is nothing more than an academic charade. But it costs the taxpayer dearly.

A taxpayer not only has to overcome the presumption of correctness of the IRS (recall Figure 1.1), he also has to prove that each alternative theory posed by the IRS is inapplicable. This is indeed a formidable burden. We summarize and portray this burden for you in Figure 11.2.

Fraud Penalty Abusiveness

There are some persons in the IRS who believe that they are absolute gods. Their word is "the law" . . . and they don't hesitate to let you know it. These persons are usually supervisors, mid-level managers, special agents, assistant district directors, criminal investigators, staff attorneys, and the like. Their practice is to intimidate a taxpayer into accepting their position on a disputed matter . . . or else.

Or else, they'll assert the civil fraud penalty (75%). Or else, the criminal fraud penalty ($100,000 fine). IRS agents and officials can do this, BASED SOLELY ON THEIR OWN PERSONAL WHIMS! There are no objective guidelines in the tax code or regulations defining fraud or enumerating its indicia.

You don't believe this, of course. "The IRS wouldn't be so rash," you say to yourself. "After all, it is supposed to abide by the law." Really? Let us cite the law for you. It is Section 7454(a): *Burden of Proof in Fraud*; it reads as follows:

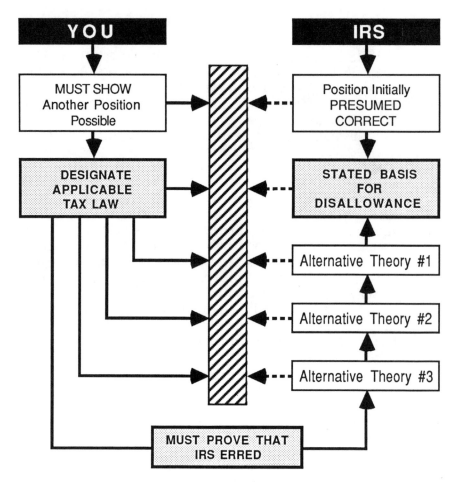

Fig. 11.2 - The "Burden of Proof" Hurdle for Taxpayers

In any proceeding involving the issue whether the petitioner has been guilty of fraud with intent to evade tax, the burden of proof in respect of such issue shall be upon the [IRS].

Note the phrase: "in any proceeding." This means that the IRS does not have to prove fraud unless a taxpayer petitions the Tax Court to make it prove its allegations. In the meantime, any IRS employee can threaten and assert the fraud penalties any time he or she wants. There is no internal supervision; no check-off list of criteria; no in-depth investigation of the alleged fraudulent act(s); and no constraints against the accuser. This is shameful tax administration.

To illustrate the abusiveness of the fraud penalty, we paraphrase Exhibit 59-BG presented in Tax Court cases 8579-88 and 28098-88. It is a "conversation" between an IRS agent and an uncowered taxpayer. It goes—

> IRS Agent: *We're getting sick and tired of you taxpayers around here. You're playing games with the system.*
> Taxpayer: "I made a good faith, one-time, unconditional public gift of my Social Security benefits forever."
> IRS Agent: *There was no gift. You whole idea is outrageous, preposterous, and frivolous. So much so that we are going to recommend the civil fraud penalty against you.*
> Taxpayer: "There are no elements of fraud here. Fraud requires concealment with intent to evade. There has been no concealment of any kind."
> IRS Agent: *It doesn't matter. You have willfulness here: 3 years in a row. So we are going to recommend the fraud penalty for each of those 3 years. There was an understatement of tax each year.*
> Taxpayer: "I'm entitled to a charitable deduction under Section 170 of the tax code."
> IRS Agent: *Section 170 doesn't apply here; it never did and it never will.*
> Taxpayer: "Section 170(c) uses the phrase "exclusively for public purposes.'"
> IRS Agent: *That doesn't apply either. I'm going to warn you right now: If you persist in claiming a charitable deduction for this, I guarantee you I'll turn this over to our Criminal Investigation Division and recommend the criminal fraud penalty in addition to the civil fraud penalty.*

You get the point, don't you?

When power perverts in the IRS want to throw their weight around, they scream the fraud penalty at you. Do you see any good faith, objective analysis by the IRS agent above? No; it was just that one agent's word. Incidentally, the IRS agent could **not** prove his fraud allegations in Tax Court. Nevertheless, it cost the petitioner $92,000 in attorney fees to combat this kind of IRS abusiveness.

Tax Court Pros & Cons

By far, most tax disputes wind up in Tax Court rather than in Claims Court or District Court. There are practical reasons for this. The foremost reason is that the Notice of Deficiency (recall Figure 8.1) issued by the IRS gives you no other choice. You either pay the tax asserted or contest the matter in Tax Court.

On this point, the official deficiency notice says—

If you want to contest this deficiency in court before making any payment, you have 90 days from the above mailing date of this letter . . . to file a petition with the United States Tax Court for a redetermination of the deficiency.

The primary advantage of Tax Court is that the court **must accept** jurisdiction of your case. The IRS cannot motion the court for dismissal for lack of jurisdiction, lack of cause, or lack of substance. When you seek jurisdiction in Claims Court or District Court, the IRS, through its legal associates in the Department of Justice, constantly hammers at these courts for dismissal. The IRS can't do this in Tax Court. The Tax Court has to accept your case.

Another advantage is that all the IRS's collection enforcement proceedings are automatically suspended. The period of suspension commences upon the date of filing (and docketing) your petition and ends on the date of the final decision on your case. This frees you from the worry about liens, levies, and seizures.

A third advantage is that there is a "calendar call" by the court on the IRS (as well as on you). This means that the IRS cannot drag out its case endlessly. Typically, the maximum duration of a Tax Court case — from time of petition to time of decision — is two to three years.

A fourth advantage is that Tax Court judges have more specialized experience in tax matters than most other federal judges. They can focus better on the core issue(s) and can relate more directly to prior Tax Court cases involving similar issues. There are no juries to play to or to instruct.

There are also disadvantages to Tax Court proceedings. Probably the most troublesome is that most said judges are ex-IRS officials and attorneys. If they are not appointed from the IRS, they are appointed from other federal agencies which have tax and legal divisions, such as: Department of Justice, Social Security Administration, Department of Labor, etc. While the Tax Court is an independent agency of its own, there is a "brother agency" syndrome favoring the IRS in close-call cases.

Another disadvantage is that there is no suspension of the running of statutory interest on any redetermined tax deficiency. The IRS should long ago have prevailed upon Congress to suspend statutory interest in parallel with suspension of its collection enforcement. However, the IRS did prevail upon Congress to prohibit a taxpayer from claiming statutory interest as a deduction on his subsequent year return(s).

The primary disadvantage of the Tax Court is that it cannot deal with other than pure tax deficiency matters. As to matters of impropriety, misconduct, and misbehavior by the IRS prior to, during, or following its proceedings, the Tax Court is useless. It acts more like a protective shield for the IRS. It shies away from ever disciplining that agency. The Tax Court, however, can discipline and fine a taxpayer on the slightest pretext.

There are other pros and cons of the Tax Court system. We do our best to summarize them in Figure 11.3. The long and short of our summary is that if there is a pure tax dispute, without any IRS abusiveness, the Tax Court is your best litigious forum.

Section 7430 Says—

Inexperienced litigants (taxpayers *and* their attorneys) are misled when they read Section 7430 of the tax code. This section is titled: *Awarding of Costs and Certain Fees.* Its substance is expressed in subsection (a) which reads (in part)—

> *The prevailing party **may be** awarded a judgment or a settlement for—*
> *(1) reasonable administrative costs incurred in connection with such administrative proceeding **within** the [IRS], and*
> *(2) reasonable litigation costs incurred in connection with such court proceeding.* [Emphasis added.]

Subsection 7430(c)(4)(A) defines the term "prevailing party" as—

> *Any party in any proceeding to which subsection (a) applies (other than the [IRS])—*
> *(i) which has substantially prevailed with respect to the **amount** in controversy, or*

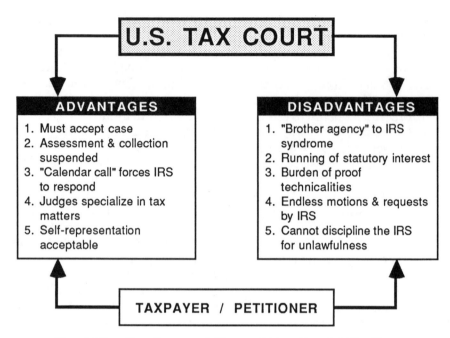

Fig. 11.3 - The Pros and Cons of Tax Court Litigation

(ii) which has substantially prevailed with respect to the most significant issue or set of issues presented, and (iii) which meets the requirements of 28 USC 2412 (d)(1)(B) [regarding net worth less than $2,000,000 for separate individuals ($4,000,000 for married individuals)].

Pursuant to subsection 7430(c)(4)(B), the "prevailing party" is *the IRS* if its position is *substantially justified* by following *its* applicable published guidelines.

What is Section 7430 really saying?

It says that if you "substantially prevailed" in your litigation with the IRS, you MAY BE awarded reasonable attorney fees (at $110/hour) and reasonable administrative costs (at IRS rates). To be awarded these fees and costs, you must **additionally prove** that:

1. You "exhausted" the administrative remedies and appeals within the IRS.

2. The position of the IRS (at the time of its Appeals Office decision or at time of its Notice of Deficiency) was not substantially justified by not following its own rules.
3. Your net worth as an individual is less than $2,000,000.
4. You applied to the IRS for fees and costs within 90 days of its administrative decision.
5. You applied to the Tax Court (or other applicable court) within 90 days of its judicial decision.

Can you imagine the reception you'll get when applying to the IRS — or to the Tax Court — for awarding you attorney fees and costs, even if you win hands down?

The IRS and the Tax Court will fight you every step of the way. The record on awarding attorney fees and costs to prevailing taxpayers is dismal. Through the end of 1997, approximately 700 applications have been made; less than 50 have been awarded. The IRS and the courts have shown little propensity to honor the spirit of Section 7430. This is all because the statute says: MAY BE awarded, instead of "shall be" awarded. The result is that Section 7430 is totally discretionary. It has nothing to do with the merits of prevailing.

Claims Court Jurisdiction

The major disadvantage of Tax Court is that the proceedings can drag on interminably. Too often, the time between the origin of a dispute and its resolution can take three to five years. It can actually take longer, if one appeals within the IRS (as discussed in Chapter 7) before going into Tax Court. In some situations, a better alternative is to proceed into the *U.S. Court of Federal Claims* (formerly the U.S. Claims Court), also referred to as the "Court of Claims."

The Claims Court has its principal office in Washington, D.C. (National Courts Building, 717 Madison Place, 20005). It is fundamentally a "paper court" where judgments are rendered primarily on documentation and its relevance to applicable tax law. It is not a jury court; it has its own rules of procedure; it requires a filing fee of $120; and pro se cases (without attorney) can be heard. Only in rare tax cases is appearance for testimony under oath needed. When testimony is needed, it is taken at a Federal Building in a city nearest to the taxpayer plaintiff's residence. In all cases, the *United States* — **not** the IRS — is your defendant. This means that Department of Justice attorneys (U.S. attorneys) take on the same adversarial role against you that IRS attorneys do in Tax Court proceedings.

To familiarize you with the jurisdictional scope of the Claims Court, we quote from Section 1436(a)(1) of the Judicial Code. It reads in part as—

*The Court of Federal Claims shall have jurisdiction of any civil action against the United States for the **recovery of any** internal revenue tax alleged to have been **erroneously or illegally** assessed or collected, or any penalty claimed to have been collected without authority or **any sum** alleged to have been excessive or **in any manner** wrongfully collected under internal revenue laws.* [Emphasis added.]

Therefore, one can seek in Claims Court the recovery of any amount of tax, penalty, or other sum which he claims was erroneously assessed and collected by the IRS. To recover any such amount, however, one must have *prepaid* the disputed amount in full. In other words, all tax claims in the Claims Court are **refund** claims. A "refund," if granted, is the return of an overpayment of some kind.

On this point, Section 6532(a) of the IR Code: *Suits by Taxpayers for Refund*, says—

*No suit or proceeding . . . for the recovery of any . . . sum, shall be begun **before the expiration of 6 months** from the date of filing the claim* [first, with the IRS].

Thus, you pay the disputed amount up front, file a claim for its refund with the IRS, and then if no response within six months, you file a claim with the U.S. Court of Federal Claims. This is a much shorter period than going through the IRS appeals process and then into Tax Court. The disadvantage is that you have to pay the disputed amount up front. By doing so, you save three to five years of statutory interest that otherwise would accrue through the Tax Court process.

District Court Jurisdiction

You cannot institute a lawsuit against an IRS officer, agent, or employee in the Claims Court. If you have a complaint against such a person for violating your rights, you must file your action in a U.S. District Court. Your defendant is the entire U.S. Government: not a particular IRS person, though such person may be named as a collateral defendant. Here, again, U.S. attorneys from the Justice Department will be your adversaries.

District Courts have a broad jurisdictional charter. They can address *any federal question* arising under the U.S. Constitution, any Act of Congress, or any regulation or procedure of the IRS. There is a U.S. District Court in every city where there is a Federal Building.

Technically, a District Court has "concurrent jurisdiction" with the Claims Court on tax refund matters. As a practical matter, however, District Courts prefer that all refund disputes be handled by the Claims Court or by the Tax Court. It is a matter of jurisdictional specialties, as depicted in Figure 11.4. Of the three, only the District Court has the authority to impanel a jury.

As you will see in the next chapter, there are certain sections of the Internal Revenue Code where you must file your action in a District Court and no other. When doing so, the procedures are quite formal. The *Federal Rules of Civil Procedure* require that one copy of your complaint be served legally upon the U.S. Attorney, Department of Justice, in the Federal Building where District Court nearest to you is located. Another copy is to be sent (by certified mail) to the Attorney General in Washington, D.C. Because of the extreme formality of such procedures, we strongly urge that you engage a knowledgeable attorney. Any attempt at pro se (self representation) will get short shrift.

We also caution you that, before filing suit in District Court, your complaint be well focused and clearly within a specific statute affecting internal revenue. Quote the key words of each applicable section and subsection as the basis for your cause of action. Even when you do this, the U.S. Attorney's required Answer will deny everything; will contain boiler plate Affirmative Defenses; and will include a Motion to Dismiss. The Motion will assert that you failed to state a proper cause of action, even though you took great pains to make it proper.

By far the greatest use of a District Court is by the IRS (USA) against taxpayers. On this, Section 1345 (Judicial Code) says—

Except as otherwise provided by Act of Congress, the District Courts shall have original jurisdiction of all civil actions, suits, or proceedings commenced by the United States, or by any agency or officer thereof expressly authorized to sue by Act of Congress. [Emphasis added.]

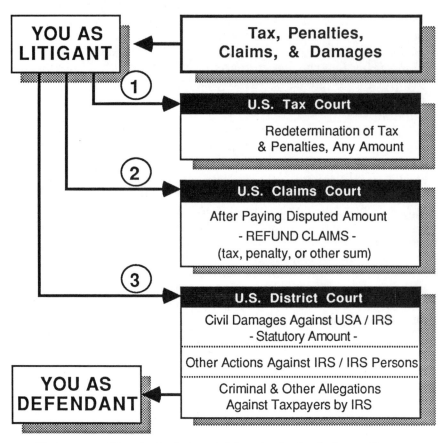

Fig. 11.4 - The Jurisdictional "Specialties" of Court Forums

The IRS cannot initiate action in Tax Court; it can, but seldom does, in Claims Court. This leaves the District Court as the primary forum for the IRS's action against defiant taxpayers who rely on their constitutional rights. Anyone doing so is automatically classed as a "tax protester." The truly sad thing about our tax system is the underlying contempt that the IRS has towards the Constitution of the United States.

12

SUING IRS AGENTS

It Is Common Knowledge That IRS Agents Can Abuse Their Discretion And Cause Irreversible Economic Harm To Taxpayers. When So, A Complaint For Damages Can Be Filed In Any U.S. District Court Naming The United States As Defendant And The Offending IRS Person(s) As Collateral Defendant(s). Triable Offenses Include Unauthorized Inspection Or Disclosure Of Returns And Return Information, Failure To Release Lien, Unauthorized Collection Actions, And Other IRS Wrongdoings. When A Taxpayer Plaintiff Prevails (Or Partially Prevails), Court Costs And Attorney Fees May Be Awarded.

For nearly 60 years (since 1939), delinquent taxpayers have been damaged, distressed, and destroyed by IRS agents "enforcing the law." For nearly 60 years, injured taxpayers have tried to sue the responsible IRS agents on constitutional grounds. For nearly 60 years, the courts (U.S. District Courts and U.S. Appeals Courts) have held steadfastly to the principle of *sovereign immunity* of the IRS and its agents. For nearly 60 years, financially damaged and emotionally injured taxpayers have had to suffer and endure, and make the best of the IRS abuses heaped upon them.

A good example of the prior futility of trying to sue an IRS agent is IRC Section 7214. This section is titled: *Offenses by Officers and Employees of the United States*. Its subsection (a) is titled: *Unlawful Acts of Revenue Officers or Agents*. The gist is—

Any officer or employee of the [IRS] *acting in connection with any revenue law—*

>   *(1) who is guilty of any extortion or willful oppression under color of law; or*
>   *(2) who knowingly demands other or greater sums than are authorized by law; or*
>   *[(3) through (9)]*

>   *shall be dismissed from office or discharged from employment and, upon conviction thereof, shall be fined not more than $10,000, or imprisoned not more than 5 years, or both.*

This law, Section 7214, has been on the books since 1939. It has been amended only twice: each involving only a minor editorial change. Yet, through the end of 1997, only 18 cases have been heard. Of the 18, only three have resulted in convictions. The first conviction was in 1956 [*E.T. Waldin*, (DC) 56-1 USTC ¶ 9347; 138 F Supp 791]; the second conviction was in 1957 [*J.J. Connelly*, CA-8, 57-2 USTC ¶ 10,029; 249 F2d 576]; and the third conviction was in 1968 [*P. Branker*, CA-2, 68-1 USTC ¶ 9376, 395 F2d 881]. Since these early years, the courts have turned a deaf ear to all taxpayer suits against IRS agents based on Section 7214 alone.

In 1988 (Taxpayer Rights Act 1) and again in 1996 (Taxpayer Rights Act 2), Congress finally got the futility message of Section 7214. It amended a few prior laws and added a few new ones to put "teeth" into a taxpayer's right to sue IRS agents, officials, and employees. Any cause of action cited in one's complaint must be bona fide, and directed clearly at a verifiable *unauthorized act* of the IRS person(s) charged.

In this our final chapter, we want to review the Rights Acts law changes, and cite a few cases (post-1989) where a taxpayer has won. If you've been so damaged and so incensed that you want to sue an IRS official directly, you should have some inkling of what your winning prospects might be. Be forewarned, however, that the courts still bend over backwards to protect IRS officials who allege that they are following "published procedures" within the IRS.

Confidentiality of Returns

When suing an IRS agent, one must designate a *cause of action* for each wrongful act that the agent is alleged to have committed. The most acceptable type of cause of action is where there is an express statement in the Tax Code that prohibits the agent(s) from doing what he/she/they did. One example of an express prohibition is Section 6103: *Confidentiality and Disclosure of Returns and Return Information.* Its general rule, subsection (a), states—

Returns and return information shall be confidential, and except as authorized [herein]—

> *no officer or employee of the United States, . . .shall disclose any return or return information obtained by him in any manner in connection with his service as such an officer or employee or . . . a former officer or employee.* [Emphasis added.]

This seems pretty clear enough: no IRS person shall disclose a taxpayer's tax information to persons or entities who are not otherwise authorized to receive it. Consequently, if you believe that an IRS person has publicly disclosed tax information or misinformation about you, you have a valid cause for complaint.

As to the definition of "returns" and "return information," subsection 6103(b) says, in part—

(1) The term "return" means any tax or information return, declaration of estimated tax or claim for refund . . . filed with the [IRS] . . . and any amendment or supplement thereto, including supporting schedules, attachments, or lists which are part of the return so filed.

(2) The term "return information" means a taxpayer's identity, the nature, source, or amount of his income, payments, receipts, deductions, exemptions, credits, assets, liabilities, net worth, tax liability, tax withheld, deficiencies, overassessments, or tax

payments, whether the taxpayer's return was, is being, or will be examined or subject to other investigation or processing. . . .

As you can see, the definitions of "returns" and "return information" are broad and specific. This means that if you are going to allege the wrongful disclosure of your tax information by an IRS agent, you must be equally specific as to what, where, when, how, how much, by whom, and the express dollar damage you suffered as a consequence thereof. Furthermore, you have to allege that the disclosure was willfully done with the intent to damage or defame you. If your allegations are emotional and speculative, the Justice Department attorney representing the accused IRS agent would move to have your case dismissed. Even if the specificity of your allegations is "right on," Justice Department attorneys will move for dismissal as a matter of routine.

Sample Court Rulings

Section 6103 has been one of the most litigated sections of the Internal Revenue Code. There are nearly 1,000 published rulings of which approximately 100 are post-1989 rulings. For instructional balance, we'll cite three rulings in which the taxpayer lost, and three rulings in which the taxpayer won. We must confess, though, that fewer than 10% of all cases heard are favorable to the taxpayer. We think there is a reason for this. Our belief is that there is an inherent judicial bias against any taxpayer suing an IRS agent. After all, the IRS **is** a source of revenue for judges' salaries, pensions, and health benefits. You, too, may sense this bias in the rulings below.

In *T.L. Jones* [DC Neb., 95-2 USTC ¶ 50,567], the court ruled that—

> The government was not liable for damages due to the unauthorized disclosure of information regarding the execution of a search warrant to be served on the taxpayer because the disclosure, though not exempt under Code Sec. 6103(k)(6) as an investigative disclosure, resulted from a good faith but erroneous interpretation of Code Sec. 6103.

Here, the taxpayer lost.

In *D.P. Venen* [CA-3, 94-2 USTC ¶ 50,177], the court ruled that—

> The IRS did not improperly disclose return information, even though the levy it sought to enforce was defective. The history and structure of Code Sec. 6103 indicates that the disclosure provision and the attendant remedy are distinct from and were not intended to interfere with collection actions. If unlawful levies were the basis for disclosure liability, IRS agents could face an undue burden on [their] collection authority.

Here, again, the taxpayer lost.

In *R.K. Wilkerson* [CA-5, 95-2 USTC ¶ 50,569], the court ruled that—

> A sole-proprietor's claim for damages from an unauthorized disclosure of tax return information was dismissed because the disclosure was not wrongful under Code Sec. 6103. The disclosure of her social security number, business interest, employee identification number, and alleged tax liability were necessary to provide effective notice to persons dealing with the taxpayer and her trailer manufacturing business. Even though the IRS wrongfully levied on the taxpayer's assets, such levy did not automatically constitute a wrongful disclosure.

Still, again, the taxpayer lost.

In *B.M. Barrett, Jr. M.D.* [DC Tex., 96-1 USTC ¶ 50,082], the court ruled that—

> A plastic surgeon was entitled to receive only statutory damages resulting from the IRS's disclosure of his return information, but was not entitled to actual damages or punitive damages. Even though the IRS agent acted in bad faith, the use of the words "Criminal Investigation Division" in the body of circular letters to the surgeon's patients, was not such a flagrant violation of Code Sec. 6103 that it rose to the level of being willful or grossly negligent.

Here, the taxpayer won, but only to a limited extent.

In *S. McLarty* [DC Min., 92-1 USTC ¶ 50,094, 784 F Supp 1401], the court ruled that—

> An IRS agent and an Assistant U.S. Attorney (Justice Department) were liable for wrongful disclosure of the tax returns of an attorney who

wished to represent one individual being prosecuted for criminal tax violations where the attorney was not a party to the proceedings. The IRS agent wrongfully released the attorney's tax information to the Ass't. U.S. Attorney who, in turn, disclosed the information to the U.S. District Court judge assigned to the case. Thereafter, the attorney's application for admission to defend the individual was denied. Such disclosure was not authorized under Code Sec. 6103 and it violated the attorney's clearly established statutory right to the confidentiality of his return information.

Here, the taxpayer won, but he had to allege separate violations against the IRS agent, the Ass't. U.S. Attorney, **and** a U.S. District Court judge.

In *E.E. Johnson* [DC Tex., 96-2 USTC ¶ 50,337], the court ruled that—

An insurance company executive who brought suit against various IRS employees for their improper public disclosures of return information (his identity, title, address, and nature of tax dispute) which caused him to lose his job, was awarded damages pursuant to a jury verdict in his favor. "Because of the unmitigated arrogance and unprofessional conduct of the U.S. attorney," the amount of the award was $600,000.

Here, the taxpayer clearly won, but it was at the expense of losing his job, to which he was not reinstated.

Again With "Teeth"

Of the nearly 1,000 Section 6103 cases heard, less than 10% (closer to 5% actually) were taxpayer wins or partial wins. When you're made aware of the entirety of Section 6103, you will understand why violated taxpayers do so poorly. The statute consists of approximately 16,000 words — **yes, the count is 16,000** (approximately). Previously, we've cited only about 150 of its words. It is not a confidentiality law: it is a **disclosure** law. Its title (again) is: Confidentiality AND Dislosure of Returns and Return Information. The result is that only 150 words are devoted to confidentiality, whereas over 15,000 words are devoted to authorized disclosures. The authorized disclosures are the exceptions to confidentiality. As the judicial rationale indicates, the

IRS must be granted so many exceptions because . . . *taxes are the lifeblood of government* [*Battley v US*, CA-9 Aug 14, 1997].

Lifeblood or not, the 1988 and 1996 Rights Acts have enacted two laws with some "teeth" in them. The two are:

Sec. 7213   —   *Unauthorized Disclosure of Information*
Sec. 7213A   —   *Unauthorized Inspection of Returns or Return Information*

Section 7213 consists of about 850 words: Section 7213A about 170. Section 7213 was first enacted in 1954, but has been amended 18 times! It was most recently amended on August 5, 1997 at which time Section 7213A was enacted.

The primary thrust of Section 7213 is its subsection (a)(1): *Returns and Return Information*; *Federal Employees*. Its key wording reads as—

It shall be unlawful for any officer or employee of the U.S. . . . or any former officer or employee, willfully to disclose to any person, except as authorized [in section 6103], *any return or return information (as defined in section 6103(b)). Any violation of this paragraph shall be a felony punishable upon conviction by fine in any amount not exceeding $5,000, or imprisonment of not more than 5 years, or both, together with the costs of prosecution.*

The thrust of Section 7213A is its short subsections (a): *Prohibitions*, and (b): *Penalty*. Combining these two subsections, the gist is—

It shall be unlawful for any officer or employee of the U.S. . . . willfully to inspect, except as authorized, any return or return information acquired by such person . . . under a provision of section 6103.

Any violation of subsection (a) shall be punishable upon conviction by a fine in an amount not exceeding $1,000 or *imprisonment of not more than 1 year, or both, together with the costs of prosecution.*

From a casual reading of these two IR Code sections, it appears as though real teeth have been added to protect violated taxpayers. It certainly appears this way. But have the "teeth" really worked? It may be too early to tell. As to Section 7213, there are only about 35 published court rulings: none is a clear-cut taxpayer victory. As to Section7213A, because of its brand newness, there are as yet no published rulings.

Two Particular Sec. 7213 Rulings

Despite the above, there are two particular Section 7213 rulings that we want to tell you about. They are what we call "most interesting" cases because they reveal the vindictiveness of IRS agents who have been sued. Even if you sue an IRS agent and win, your litigation problems don't end there.

Our first revealing case is that of *L.M. Richey* [CA-9, 91-1 USTC ¶ 50,055; 924 F2d 857]. *Richey* was a former IRS agent for 25 years, and retired to engage in his own private tax practice. While as an agent, he audited an attorney's tax return and found deficiencies in that return. The attorney promptly paid the additional tax assessed. Later, the attorney became a District Court Judge (*McDonald*).

In the course of Judge McDonald's presidings, *Richey*, in his private practice, was charged with conspiracy in the preparation of false and fraudulent tax returns. McDonald's jury found *Richey* guilty as charged. He was sentenced to a term of probation and enjoined from making derogatory remarks about the U.S. Government. This probation condition attracted much press attention. In various press interviews, *Richey* let it be known that he had audited one of Judge McDonald's returns and found discrepancies in it. *Richey* thereafter postulated that his conviction was the sole result of McDonald's judicial bias.

The Appellate Court upheld *Richey's* original conviction by ruling that—

Although the former agent had a substantial interest in a fair trial and a right to comment upon matters of public concern, such as judicial bias, this did not outweigh the compelling government interest to provide a confidential and workable tax system.

In another bizarre case, that of *R.L. Marré* [CA-5 Jul 22, 1997; 97-2 USTC ¶ 50,573], the taxpayer, upon appeal, won a wrongful disclosure award. The District Court awarded *Marré* $1,000 in statutory damage for each of the IRS agent's **215 unauthorized disclosures** ($215,000). The court also awarded reasonable attorneys' fees and costs totaling $326,000.

While *Marré's* case was being heard, the IRS assessed him $2,000,000 ($2 million) for promoting alleged abusive tax shelters. In the belief that Marré was marketing modular solar-heated greenhouses fraudulently, the Criminal Investigation Division (CID) of the IRS began an investigation. It sent out 215 circular letters to investors and suppliers that *Marré* was under investigation by the CID, and that his operation was false and fraudulent. Attached to each letter was a questionnaire couched with statements that *Marré* was dishonest with his investors.

The court issue was whether the IRS could refuse to pay *Marré* any damages at all. The IRS argued that it had the authority to offset the entire award $541,000 (215,000 + 326,000) against the $2,000,000 tax assessment. The correctness of the $2,000,000 was not resolved. However, the court did rule that the IRS could use the $215,000 as an offset, but not the $326,000 in attorneys' fees. The court concluded that the attorneys' fees belonged to the attorneys: not to the prevailing taxpayer.

Attorney fee awards for prosecuting unauthorized IRS acts stems from Section 7430: *Awarding of Costs and Certain Fees*. Since its inception in 1983, approximately 700 Section 7430 cases have been heard. Of this number, less than 50 have resulted in awards to taxpayers. This is an awards rate of around 7% (50 ÷ 700). This is not a significant prevailing rate for taxpayer plaintiffs who are only seeking the award of court costs and attorney fees. In reality, far more than 7% of Section 7430 cases are partial wins by taxpayers, who are not awarded any costs..

Five New Damage Laws

As we pointed out properly in Chapter 11 and again above, Section 7430 (Award of attorney fees) is a rather toothless law. Any award is entirely discretionary with the presiding judge (be it Tax Court, Claims Court, or District Court). The core of this discretionary power is the statutory phrase—

The prevailing party MAY be awarded a judgment or a settlement for . . .

Evidently, Congress — every so reluctantly — has only recently caught on to the toothlessness of Section 7430. This could explain the "rash" of five new civil damage laws recently enacted (relative to the "birth" of the IRS in 1913). The full titles and dates of enactment of these new laws are:

Sec. 7431 — *Civil Damages for Unauthorized Inspection or Disclosure of Returns and Return Information*
— TEFRA: 9-03-82
[Tax Equity & Fiscal Responsibility Act]

Sec. 7432 — *Civil Damages for Failure to Release Lien*
— TBOR1: 11-10-88
[Taxpayer Bill of Rights (Act)]

Sec. 7433 — *Civil Damages for Certain Unauthorized Collection Actions*
— TBOR1: 11-10-88

Sec. 7434 — *Civil Damages for Fraudulent Filing of Information Returns*
— TBOR2: 7-30-96

Sec. 7435 — *Civil Damages for Unauthorized Enticement of Information Disclosure*
— TBOR2: 7-30-96

See Figure 12.1 for a thumbnail sketch of the differences.

ITEM	IR CODE SECTIONS				
	7431	7432	7433	7434	7435
Short Title	Un-authorized Inspection or Disclosure	Failure to Release Lien	Un-authorized Collection Actions	False Information Returns	Un-authorized Enticement of Information
Effective Date	9-03-83	11-10-88	11-10-88	7-30-96	7-30-96
Maximum Damages	$1,000 each act plus punitive damages	Actual damages sustained	$1,000,000 (1 million)	Actual damages sustained	Actual damages sustained
Exceptions Limitations	Good faith but erroneous in-terpretations	Must exhaust ad-ministration remedies	Award reduced if no mitigation effort	File copy of complaint with IRS	Information re crimes & frauds
Time for Bringing Action	2 yrs. after discovery	2 yrs. after "right of action" accrues	2 yrs. after "right of action" accrues	1 yr. after discovery (otherwise 6 yrs.)	2 yrs. after discovery
Court Costs	Yes	Yes	Yes	Yes	Yes
Attorney Fees	Court's discretion	Sec. 7430	Sec. 7430	Court's discretion	None, if penalty imposed
Cases Heard (thru 1996)	Approx. 125	Approx. 35	Approx. 80	None	None

Fig. 12.1 - Synopsis of 5 "New" Tax Laws for Civil Damage Claims

In contrast to the 3,000 statutory words of Section 7430, all of these new sections are relatively short. They range between 300 words to about 500 words (for Section 7431). Also in contrast to Section 7430, all five of the above sections include the same mandatory phrase—

Upon a finding of liability on the part of the defendant, the defendant [the United States] *SHALL be liable to the plaintiff* [taxpayer] *in an amount of . . .*

The awardable civil damage amount is couched in such terms as *... the greater/lesser of $_____ or the sum of.* The "sum of" phrase includes (1) *actual, direct economic damages sustained by the plaintiff* [plus] (2) *the costs of the action.*

As is clearly indicated in Figure 12.1, the number of actual court rulings on Sections 7431 through 7435 is quite low. This, of course, is due to their relative newness. As you can also see in Figure 12.1, there are (as yet) no published rulings on Sections 7434 and 7435. Consequently, we can offer no instructive commentary on these latest two new sections. We will, however, provide commentary below separately on Section 7431, Section 7432, and Section 7433.

All causes of action under Sections 7431 through 7435 must be filed in a U.S. District Court. With the exception of Section 7434 (false information returns), this means that your defendant is the entire United States government. The defendant is **not** the perpetrating IRS agent or agents, though said persons can, and should be named among the "et als." The fact that IRS agents are not named as the primary defendant probably eases the backlashing stings of retaliation and vindictiveness by said agents. Any damage awards granted come out of the "government's pockets": not out of the personal pockets of the IRS wrongdoers.

Commentary on Section 7431

The general rule under Section 7431 (Unauthorized Inspection or Disclosure) reads in part as—

*If any officer or employee of the United States **knowingly, or by reason of negligence,** inspects or discloses any return or return information with respect to a taxpayer in violation of any provision of section 6103 [re Confidentiality, etc.], such taxpayer may bring a civil action for damages **against the United States.** . . . [Emphasis added.]*

Exceptions. *No liability shall arise under this section with respect to any inspection or disclosure . . . which results from a good faith, but erroneous, interpretation of section 6103.*

Of the approximately 125 rulings under Section 7431, approximately 40 or about 32% [40 ÷ 125] can be classed as taxpayer wins or partial wins. In all of the clear winning cases, the plaintiff taxpayer alleged properly that

1. One or more IRS agents acted "knowingly or negligently" in their unauthorized inspections or disclosures.

2. Such unauthorized acts were not the result of "good faith but erroneous" interpretations.

3. The unauthorized acts were committed within 2 years after date of discovery.

It is significant to be aware that there is no "less than" $2,000,000 net worth statement to qualify a cause of action, as there is with Section 7430 (Award of attorney fees). The no net worth statement requirement also applies to Sections 7432 through 7435. This absence of net worth statement as a cause of action probably accounts for a third of the additional winnings under Section 7431 as opposed to Section 7430.

Additionally, Section 7431 provides for the award of *punitive* damages. None of the other four sections contains a punitive damages clause. On this point, subsection 7431(c): ***Damages***, reads in part—

> *Upon a finding of liability* . . . [the amount of damages] ***shall be*** *. . . an amount* ***equal to the sum of***—
>
> *(1) the* ***greater of***—
>
>   *(A) $1,000 for each act of unauthorized inspection or disclosure . . . or,*
>
>   *(B) the* ***sum*** *of*—
>   *(i) the actual damages sustained by the plaintiff . . . , plus*
>   *(ii) in the case of a willful inspection or disclosure or an inspection or disclosure which*

> *is the result of gross negligence, **punitive** damages, plus*
> *(2) the costs of the action.* [Emphasis added.]

Presumably the clause "costs of the action" could include attorney fees. Such is not explicitly stated nor prohibited. Ordinarily, however, the term "costs" in litigative matters includes all court procedural costs *other than* attorney fees. The reason for this distinction is that attorney fees are negotiable whereas direct court costs are not.

At *minimum*, therefore, a finding of liability induces an award of $1,000 for each unauthorized act, plus associated court costs. As to any punitive damages, we can hear the affected IRS agents screaming their bloody heads off about sovereign immunity and *their* constitutional rights. All wrongfully aggressive IRS agents share a common blind spot: *they* have constitutional rights, but you as a taxpayer do not.

Commentary on Section 7432

Section 7432: *Civil Damages for Failure to Release Lien*, thrusts directly at Section 6325: *Release of Lien or Discharge of Property*. Section 6325 sets the conditions for the release of a lien. When the conditions are met (liability satisfied or unenforceable, or bond accepted), the IRS must release the lien or face the awarding of damages. Whereas Section 7432 consists of about 300 words, Section 6325 consists of about 1,260 words. Thus, when a wronged taxpayer is contemplating action under Section 7432, he and his attorney must familiarize themselves with Section 6325.

Furthermore, before filing a suit under Section 7432, the taxpayer must—

1. Establish that he has exhausted administrative remedies available within the IRS.
2. Show that he made all reasonable effort to mitigate the damage through correction actions on his part.
3. Notify the IRS of its failure to release the lien; such "notice date" becomes one's date of right to action.

The purpose of these requirements is to reduce the amount of litigation attacking the IRS's most used enforcement tool: that of filing a Federal Tax Lien. As we implied in Chapters 9 and 10, the IRS is not required to notify a taxpayer when a lien has been filed. Yet, when a taxpayer discovers the lien, and has met the conditions of Section 6325, he has to notify the IRS of its failure to release the lien. Why does Congress let the IRS stack everything in its favor?

Nevertheless, the general rule of Section 7432(a) reads in pertinent part—

If any officer or employee of the Internal Revenue Service knowingly, or by reason of negligence, fails to release a lien under section 6325 . . . such taxpayer may bring a civil action for damages. . . .

Particularly note that the IRS is expressly identified. Contrast this to "any officer or employee of the United States" in Section 7431. Obviously, Section 7432 applies only to officers and employees of the IRS; they are the only government agents that can issue and execute a Federal Tax Lien.

The statutory damages that are awardable, upon a finding of liability on the part of the IRS—

Shall be . . . equal to the sum of—

(1) actual, direct economic damages sustained by the plaintiff which, but for the actions of the defendant, would not have been sustained, plus

(2) the costs of the action.

Note that no specific dollar amount is set. Evidently, Congress felt that different taxpayers would be (or could be) damaged differently, depending on the value of their property liened upon. Besides, IRS Regulation 301.7432–1(c)(1) says—

Only actual pecuniary [monetary] damages sustained [are considered]. Injuries such as inconvenience, emotional distress, and loss of reputation are compensable only to the extent that they result in actual pecuniary damages.

Subregulation 1(d) defines "costs of the action" as filing fees, clerk fees, court reporter costs, witness fees, servicing fees, docket fees, and compensation of court appointed experts and interpreters. Subregulation 1(f): *Recovery of costs under section 7430*, says that—

Reasonable litigation costs, including attorney's fees, not recoverable under this section may be recoverable under section 7430.

As a concluding commentary on Section 7432, only about 35 cases have been heard. Of these, approximately seven were taxpayer wins or partial wins. This is a taxpayer prevailing rate of about 20% (7 ÷ 35).

Commentary on Section 7433

Like Section 7432 (Failure to Release Lien), Section 7433 (Unauthorized Collection Actions) is directed expressly at *any officer or employee of the IRS*. The full title to Section 7433 is: *Civil Damages for Certain Unauthorized Collection Actions*. The key word to note in this title is the term "certain" unauthorized actions. This word alone should tip you off that the prospects of winning are not great.

The concept that only "certain" actions can be judicially heard arises from subsection (a):

If, in connection with any collection of Federal tax . . ., any [IRS agent] *recklessly or intentionally disregards any provision of* [the IR Code], *or any regulation promulgated* [thereunder], *such taxpayer may bring a civil action for damages. . . .* [Emphasis added.]

Section 7433 boils down to collection enforcement misconduct, and nothing else. Furthermore, the misconduct must be "reckless" or "intentional disregard." What do these terms mean? Regulation 301.7433-1, which consists of approximately 1,700 words does **not** define these terms.

If IRS liability is found, the award of damages to a plaintiff (subsection (b))—

*Shall be . . . an amount equal to **the lesser of $1,000,000** [1 million] or the sum of—*

(1) actual, direct economic damages sustained by the plaintiff as a proximate result of the reckless or intentional action of the [IRS] officer or employee, and

(2) the costs of the action.

The court rulings in Section 7433 are not very numerous: totaling approximately 80. Of this number, taxpayer wins or partial wins are only about 10. This is a taxpayer prevailing result of about 12% (10 ÷ 80). Most of the losings were the result of the IRS "stacking the deck," regulatorily. It promulgated the regulation that its own administrative procedures be exhausted *before* any court action could be filed.

Wisely, though belatedly, Congress softened the IRS's pre-court requirement, for cases filed after July 30, 1996. The softening took the form of amending subsection 7433(d)(1): *Award for Damages May Be Reduced . . .*

if the court determines that the plaintiff has not exhausted the administrative remedies available.

The difference is that legitimate cases can go forward and be heard, instead of being summarily dismissed for not toeing the IRS line. Instead of no damages at all, reduced damages can be awarded.

Recording IRS Misconduct

With respect to Sections 7431, 7432, and 7433, the grand total number of cases heard is around 250. Of this number, only about

55 can be classed as taxpayer wins or partial wins. This is an overall civil damages prevailing rate of about 22% (55 ÷ 250). In all truthfulness, however, almost two-thirds of this 22% are partial prevailings: not full prevailings. This raises the question: Why are taxpayer plaintiffs not more successful?

Side stepping the "stacked deck" bias and burdens of proof that all taxpayers face in tax disputes, we think there is one primary reason why taxpayers are not more successful. It is the failure to record each act of IRS misconduct as it occurs. Taxpayers depend entirely on their attorneys to come up with some magic strategy to blow away the IRS and U.S. attorneys (of the Justice Department). There is just no magic substitute for an accurate recording of each IRS misconduct event.

Most violated taxpayers do not know, or do not realize, where, when, and how they are being violated. They tend to accept any abuses, mistreatments, and misassertions by the IRS as a way of life in dealing with such a powerful agency of government. Once they realize that they have been violated, they fail to take the extra effort needed to record in a diary, notebook, or log each and every misconduct event that they encounter. When it comes time to file a judicial complaint, they lack the specificity of facts that are needed to enshrine them in the statutory requirements for a valid cause of action. As a result, they make only general allegations of the wrongdoings of IRS agents. Accusing an IRS agent of harassment, malicious prosecution, coercion, intimidation, and so on is just not sufficient.

Instead, every violated taxpayer must record in whatever manner he is most comfortable with, every threat, every coercive act, every erroneous document, every item of harm, and every improper claim that an IRS agent makes against him. Record the specific date, the hour of the day, the words said, the documents filed, and any unauthorized behavior. For example, if an IRS agent verbally threatens you with "criminal investigation" if you don't immediately agree to sign some document or to pay some tax amount, he (or she) is engaging in misconduct. Or, if some agent threatens you with "assessing all the penalties" he (or she) can think of, you know you have an abusive agent on your hands. These and other suggested matters for recording care are presented in Figure 12.2.

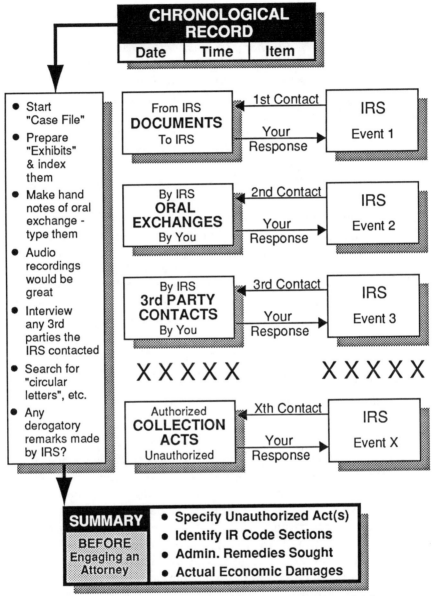

Fig. 12.2 - Steps to Take When Recording IRS's Wrongful Acts

As a wrap-up to your records, record statements from potential witnesses, and document your attempt at administrative remedies.

Once you have your facts, figures, and documents in place, decide on your own if, or which, civil damage claim law applies. Is it Section 7431: *Unauthorized Inspection or Disclosure*; is it Section 7432: *Failure to Release Lien*; or is it Section 7433: *Unauthorized Collection Actions*? To feel more confident in your position, visit your public library (tax law section), and review the full text of the IRC sections, the applicable regulations, and any relevant court rulings. Photocopy for your own records those portions of the reviewed material which fit your case. Do this before engaging an attorney.

Face it; you *will* need to engage an attorney. When doing so, remind him (or her) that your defendant is: THE UNITED STATES, and that your complaint must be filed in your nearest U.S. District Court. Mention that some Assistant U.S. Attorney (from the Department of Justice) will be the opposing attorney, and that you are aware that said attorney may be quite unethical and deceptive in his/her motions and procedures. Make sure that your attorney is familiar with the IR Code sections on which you rely, and that he verify himself your fulfillment of each cause of action thereunder. Both of you prepare for delays and shenanigans by IRS and Justice Department representatives, and their screams of "sovereign immunity" every chance they get.

Frivolous or Groundless Claims

Sovereign immunity is serious business with the IRS. It has used this club over taxpayers' heads for nearly 80 years with relative impunity. Reluctantly and begrudgingly, it has allowed Congress to make the tiniest of slices into its fortress walls. It is only through these "tiny slices" of waived immunity that a violated taxpayer has a valid cause for a damage claim. If your claim is not precisely focused (as depicted in Figure 12.3), the IRS (and Justice Department) may counterclaim that your action is *frivolous or groundless*. If the presiding judge concurs, you are in for a $10,000 surprise. Let us explain.

The prerequisites for a valid claim are signified separately on each of the above mentioned Code sections on which you rely. For example, for claims under Section 7430 (Award of attorney fees),

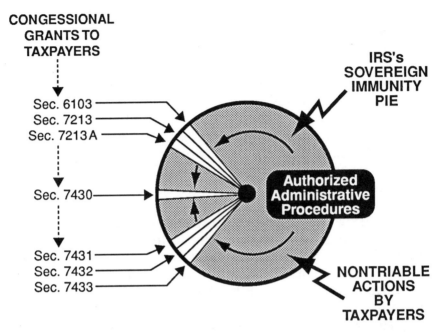

CONGESSIONAL GRANTS TO TAXPAYERS

Sec. 6103
Sec. 7213
Sec. 7213A

Sec. 7430

Sec. 7431
Sec. 7432
Sec. 7433

IRS's SOVEREIGN IMMUNITY PIE

Authorized Administrative Procedures

NONTRIABLE ACTIONS BY TAXPAYERS

Fig. 12.3 - The "Thin Slices" of Waived Sovereign Immunity of the IRS

sovereign immunity is waived only on those matters *in connection with the determination, collection, or refund of any tax, interest, or penalty* imposed under the IR Code. After which, you have the "prevailing party" issue to address.

Similarly for Section 7431 (Unauthorized inspection or disclosure) and Section 7432 (Failure to release lien). The prerequisite is that the wrongdoing IRS agent *knowingly or by reason of negligence* committed specific unauthorized acts. You have to pinpoint the wrongful act(s), while at the same time being cognizant of the authorized acts of the agent or agents. You cannot cross the line into legitimate tax administration activities.

In the case of Section 7433 (Unauthorized collection actions), the IRS foisted on Congress a real sneaker. On the surface, the prerequisites are that an abusive agent *recklessly or intentionally disregard* any provision of the IR Code or regulation thereunder. Again, you have to pinpoint the wrongful act(s) with specificity. If you don't, Section 6673 (the $10,000 surprise) comes into play. Oddly, there is no cross reference to Section 6673 in Section 7433, nor is there any cross reference to it in the 1,700-word regulation to Section 7433. One has to stumble onto Section 6673 on his own.

Section 6673 is titled: *Sanctions and Costs Awarded by Courts.* It is subsection 6673(b)(1) that is "stumble on" relevant. The title of this subsection is: *Claims under section 7433.* This subsection goes on to say—

> *Whenever it appears to the court that the taxpayer's position . . . under section 7433 is frivolous or groundless, the court may require the taxpayer to pay to the* [IRS] *a penalty not in excess of $10,000.*

In other words, if you get carried away with anger and fury towards the IRS, you may be economically damaged by the court itself. To avoid possible court-imposed damage (up to $10,000), limit your allegations to the narrow confines of each Code section on which you rely. Bear in mind also that a U.S. District Court does **not** have to hear every complaint filed with it. Nearly 50% of all plaintiff taxpayer filings are summarily dismissed. Those that survive dismissal must run the gauntlet of being bona fide and on solid ground.

ABOUT
THE AUTHOR

Holmes F. Crouch

Born on a small farm in southern Maryland, Holmes was graduated from the U.S. Coast Guard Academy with a Bachelor's Degree in Marine Engineering. While serving on active duty, he wrote many technical articles on maritime matters. After attaining the rank of Lieutenant Commander, he resigned to pursue a career as a nuclear engineer.

Continuing his education, he earned a Master's Degree in Nuclear Engineering from the University of California. He also authored two books on nuclear propulsion. As a result of the tax write-offs associated with writing these books, the IRS audited his returns. The IRS's handling of the audit procedure so annoyed Holmes that he undertook to become as knowledgeable as possible regarding tax procedures. He became a licensed private Tax Practitioner by passing an examination administered by the IRS. Having attained this credential, he started his own tax preparation and counseling business in 1972.

In the early years of his tax practice, he was a regular talk-show guest on San Francisco's KGO Radio responding to hundreds of phone-in tax questions from listeners. He was a much sought-after guest speaker at many business seminars and taxpayer meetings. He also provided counseling on special tax problems, such as divorce matters, property exchanges, timber harvesting, mining ventures, animal breeding, independent contractors, selling businesses, and offices-at-home. Over the past 25 years, he has prepared nearly 10,000 tax returns for individuals, estates, trusts, and small businesses (in partnership and corporate form).

During the tax season of January through April, he prepares returns in a unique manner. During a single meeting, he completes the return . . . *on the spot!* The client leaves with his return signed, sealed, and in a stamped envelope. His unique approach to preparing returns and his personal interest in his clients' tax affairs have honed his professional proficiency. His expertise extends through itemized deductions, computer-matching of income sources, capital gains and losses, business expenses and cost of goods, residential rental expenses, limited and general partnership activities, closely-held corporations, to family farms and ranches.

He remembers spending 12 straight hours completing a doctor's complex return. The next year, the doctor, having moved away, utilized a large accounting firm to prepare his return. Their accountant was so impressed by the manner in which the prior return was prepared that he recommended the doctor travel the 500 miles each year to have Holmes continue doing it.

He recalls preparing a return for an unemployed welder, for which he charged no fee. Two years later the welder came back and had his return prepared. He paid the regular fee . . . and then added a $300 tip.

During the off season, he represents clients at IRS audits and appeals. In one case a shoe salesman's audit was scheduled to last three hours. However, after examining Holmes' documentation it was concluded in 15 minutes with "no change" to his return. In another instance he went to an audit of a custom jeweler that the IRS dragged out for more than six hours. But, supported by Holmes' documentation, the client's return was accepted by the IRS with "no change."

Then there was the audit of a language translator that lasted two full days. The auditor scrutinized more than $1.25 million in gross receipts, all direct costs, and operating expenses. Even though all expensed items were documented and verified, the auditor decided that more than $23,000 of expenses ought to be listed as capital items for depreciation instead. If this had been enforced it would have resulted in a significant additional amount of tax. Holmes strongly disagreed and after many hours explanation got the amount reduced by more than 60% on behalf of his client.

He has dealt extensively with gift, death and trust tax returns. These preparations have involved him in the tax aspects of wills, estate planning, trustee duties, probate, marital and charitable bequests, gift and death exemptions, and property titling.

Although not an attorney, he prepares Petitions to the U.S. Tax Court for clients. He details the IRS errors and taxpayer facts by citing pertinent sections of tax law and regulations. In a recent case involving an attorney's ex-spouse, the IRS asserted a tax deficiency of $155,000. On behalf of his client, he petitioned the Tax Court and within six months the IRS conceded the case.

Over the years, Holmes has observed that the IRS is not the industrious, impartial, and competent federal agency that its official public imaging would have us believe.

He found that, at times, under the slightest pretext, the IRS has interpreted against a taxpayer in order to assess maximum penalties, and may even delay pending matters so as to increase interest due on additional taxes. He has confronted the IRS in his own behalf on five separate occasions, going before the U.S. Claims Court, U.S. District Court, and U.S. Tax Court. These were court actions that tested specific sections of the Internal Revenue Code which he found ambiguous, inequitable, and abusively interpreted by the IRS.

Disturbed by the conduct of the IRS and by the general lack of tax knowledge by most individuals, he began an innovative series of taxpayer-oriented Federal tax guides. To fulfill this need, he undertook the writing of a series of guidebooks that provide in-depth knowledge on one tax subject at a time. He focuses on subjects that plague taxpayers all throughout the year. Hence, his formulation of the "Allyear" Tax Guide series.

The author is indebted to his wife, Irma Jean, and daughter, Barbara MacRae, for the word processing and computer graphics that turn his experiences into the reality of these publications. Holmes welcomes comments, questions, and suggestions from his readers. He can be contacted in California at (408) 867-2628, or by writing to the publisher's address.

ALLYEAR Tax Guides
by Holmes F. Crouch

All of the above available at bookstores, libraries, and on the internet

For a free 8-page catalog,
or information about the above titles, contact:
ALLYEAR Tax Guides
20484 Glen Brae Drive, Saratoga, CA 95070
Phone: (408) 867-2628   Fax: (408) 867-6466